CONSIDER THE WOMEN

Consider the Women

A Provocative Guide to
Three Matriarchs of the Bible

Debbie Blue

WILLIAM B. EERDMANS PUBLISHING COMPANY
GRAND RAPIDS, MICHIGAN

Wm. B. Eerdmans Publishing Co.
4035 Park East Court SE, Grand Rapids, Michigan 49546
www.eerdmans.com

25 24 23 22 21 20 19   1 2 3 4 5 6 7

ISBN 978-0-8028-7429-0

Library of Congress Cataloging-in-Publication Data

A catalog record for this book is available from the Library of Congress.

*

Contents

Introduction   1
We Live and Die by Stories

PART ONE: ABRAHAMIC FAITH

1. Go from Your Father's House   13
   Moving to New and Unknown Places

2. Rambunctious Monotheism   18
   The Feminine Face of God

PART TWO: HAGAR

3. The Biblical Story   31
   A Matriarch on Par with a Patriarch

4. The Mother of Islam   45
   Looking for Hagar in the Qur'an,
   a Tattoo Parlor, and an Art Gallery

5. Full Faith and Effort   58
   Where I Meet a Feminist Muslim Scholar

6. Iftar   68
   Visiting a Mosque with My Daughter

PART THREE: ESTHER

7. The Biblical Story   77
   The Jewish Heroine Who Reclaims Eros

8. Purim   100
   The Farce Awakens

9. Shoah   114
   Scapegoating and Status-Seeking

PART FOUR: MARY

10. The Biblical Story   129
    The Subversive Mother of God

11. The Shape-Shifting Queen   148
    Goddesses, Guadalupe, and Grandmas

Acknowledgments   175

Notes   177

Reader's Guide and Discussion Group Questions   197

Introduction

We Live and Die by Stories

> Stories migrate secretly. The assumption that whatever we now believe is just common sense, or what we always knew, is a way to save face. It's also a way to forget the power of a story and of a storyteller, the power in the margins, and the potential for change.
>
> —Rebecca Solnit, *Hope in the Dark:*
> *Untold Histories, Wild Possibilities*

I like reading old stories—as many of them as possible—ancient Egyptian myths about a vulture-mother-goddess, Iroquois legends, the Korean story about the boy born to a fairy and a laurel tree who makes his way through high waters, saving ants and mosquitos from the flood. Or the Mayan story about the maize god resurrected from the carapace of a turtle—assisted by dwarves. I find a fascinating and expansive array of illuminating and beautiful and troubling old stories across cultures.

Old Bible Stories

But the stories that have a uniquely formative place in my life are Bible stories. I've heard them from day one—probably even in the womb. At some moments in my life, I was a bit bitter about this—what could be less sophisticated or more mundane than growing up a Baptist in Indiana? What if I had been raised by French intellectuals or Navajo elders?

At this late stage in my life I'm surprised I still spend most of my days (I'm not kidding—hours and hours) immersed in these same old Bible stories. I promise you it is not about blind loyalty. It has something to do with the fact that I'm a minister, so it's my job, but it is also that these stories seem to have an endless capacity to reveal glimpses of God, what it is to be human, things we might rather keep hidden, what is under the surface of everyday life. I am grateful for these stories that persist in baffling and nourishing me.

But I believe Scripture loses some of its capacity for revelation if we don't enter it honestly as women weary of patriarchy or as people who have seen so much injustice go down that they will never stop questioning authority. The Bible loses some of its capacity for revelation if we don't bring our questions to it. The Bible invites—almost demands—our questions.

> *These stories seem to have an endless capacity to reveal glimpses of God, what it is to be human, things we might rather keep hidden.*

Sometimes you might have to take a pitchfork to it to loosen the soil. Nothing grows in hard-packed, solid ground. Plus, using a pitchfork might just feel cathartic. Scripture has been used in so many destructive ways. It has had enormous influence throughout cultures all over the world. Bible stories are founding narratives for many people in the Jewish and Christian religions, as well as in Islam. Certain readings have produced some terrible, violently divisive theology—white supremacist, misogynist, anti-Semitic, Islamophobic, homophobic theology. Some readings have given rise to ideas about human exceptionalism that have contributed to the demise of the planet. If you want to strike the Bible with a pitchfork, I think the Merciful Lover of Creation would be okay with that.

New Stories

I know I'm not the only one feeling a bit hopeless about the state of the world. I had to pull off the interstate the other day because torrential rain was causing minor flooding. It wasn't really a big deal, but in the moment I felt furious—like, really? Can't just one little half hour go by without something happening to remind us we are doomed—violent weather, violent men, Charlottesville, North Korea, Houston, unprecedented heat, unprecedented floods, unprecedented fires, flooding on the interstate?

Lately I've been keeping the radio off when I'm in the car to try to give myself room to breathe and to be present to what is in front of me, but as I waited for the rain to let up I'm thankful I turned it on. Krista Tippett was interviewing author Rebecca Solnit. Sometimes you need to hear from someone who is smart with "a robust commitment to hope" when yours is wavering.

Rebecca was telling Krista that she thinks people in this culture "seem to love certainty more than hope" and what we need to do is let go of the certainty. The future is dark in that it is unknown. But "there is a sense of possibility in the unknown," not inevitable doom. "Love is made in the dark." If you don't know Solnit's work, she is nothing at all like a false optimist. But she believes—she has seen, she says—that in the aftermath of Katrina and other crises, disaster can move us into a place of "non-separation and compassion, and engagement and courage, . . . and generosity." Instead of falling apart, she says, we could fall together.

As I've been reading and writing about stories, I was especially alert to what she was saying. We need to think about the stories we tell and their consequences, she said. "People live and die by stories." We need more stories, better stories, more complex stories. We need to ask if there are better ways of telling our old stories and if there are stories that we fail to tell about "those players who are not in the limelight."

I started scribbling notes on an oil-change receipt so I might incorporate her words in this introduction. This book is about engaging old stories in new ways—asking questions about them, looking for hope. If the biblical stories are contributing to destruction and cruelty, if they are not helping us, then we better work on the way we are reading them and telling them. They are not going away.

One of the beautiful things about having a canon is that you can look back and see an endless matrix of interpretation unrolling over hundreds, even thousands, of years. The stories are told and retold, stretched, and excavated. They are read differently in every age—forever generating new meanings and new life for people in the times and places where they live.

I am not always fond of the way the church fathers interpreted the Bible. They had too many problems with sex, women, and Jewish people. Jerome said, "The intimacies of Mesopotamia died in the land of the Gospel," like this was a cause for celebration. He thought it was good to leave behind messy, embodied, human relationships, whereas I rather like them. The way Jerome and Tertullian and Pope Gregory the Great read the Bible had a lasting effect on the way the Christian faith developed, but clearly and luckily, the process of interpretation did not stop with them.

One of the beautiful things about having a canon is that you can look back and see an endless matrix of interpretation unrolling over hundreds, even thousands, of years.

As a preacher, I am thrilled when a scriptural passage that includes "the intimacies of Mesopotamia" turns up in the lectionary. I especially like to preach on passages that include women. This doesn't happen as often as I'd like. After the 2016 US presidential election, my church, House of Mercy, decided to create an alternative lectionary. Every week in the church year, we would preach on texts that include women—some familiar, some who never turn up in the lectionary: Mary, Miriam, Zelophehad's daughters, Mrs. Potiphar, Jephthah's daughter, Judith, and the Whore of Babylon, among others.

We did it because "people live and die by stories," and we felt a sense of urgency about finding alternative ones that might help subvert the dominant ones. The world of Scripture (and much of the history of the church and culture, politics and media, theology and philosophy—liberal and conservative) offers a mostly male narrative. We need to bring out, pay attention to, read, and reread the stories of women in the Bible (and beyond) because the status quo isn't working out very well for the majority of people on earth (people in low-lying island-nations; the Standing Rock Sioux; the Bangladeshis;

Syrian refugees; black and brown men, women, and children in the United States of White Supremacy). The status quo is not working out for the earth itself. The whole arc of the biblical narrative calls us to question the systems of power that are in place, and it gives us stories to help us do that. Yes, the dominant narrative in the Bible is the male narrative, but there are many other stories to tell.

All male narratives are not the same, obviously, and it's finally starting to sink in that what have been considered masculine and feminine characteristics are not traits that are biologically determined. But particular human ways of being that much of culture has defined as masculine have been privileged over other ways of being. We can see now that some of these have not been good for the world.

Ideas about masculinity are slowly being redefined, but many men my father's age learned that being a man meant that anger was the only acceptable emotion to display. Flaunting muscle and a violent sort of masculinity that ridicules gentleness and encourages callous displays of power was how you proved your manhood. According to this narrow definition of masculinity, a man shows love through possessiveness, rivalry, dominance, and aggression more than tenderness.

It may seem like I am being overly dramatic, but we need to rethink the ways of being that we've privileged in the past if we want life on the planet to continue. If we are fine with the life where only the one percent who can afford luxury health care and designer bomb-shelter pods (or whatever the ultrarich are preparing for the apocalypse) survive—if we are okay serving the agendas of the super-rich who get richer from climate disaster and perpetual war—then we can just keep our eyes on the dominant narrative. Otherwise, we should look for alternative ones.

I don't understand quantum physics, but I know that weak force is one of the four known fundamental interactions of nature—alongside stronger forces like electromagnetism and gravity. Jesus always seems to put the weak first—the poor, and the sick, and the meek. I trust his approach. If you value only the strong, then you don't value the weak. I know many people, men and women, who fear the revelation of their vulnerability more than almost anything. That's a narrative that needs to be transformed.

At my son's graduation from college this spring, the faculty speaker, Uditi Sen, urged the graduates to "dream up the unmaking of the world as it is." That's what I'm talking about: new stories, more stories, old stories retold in new ways. The commencement speaker, Princeton University professor Keeanga-Yamahtta Taylor, said, "The president of the United States—the most powerful politician in the world—is a racist, sexist megalomaniac. It is not a benign observation but has meant tragic consequences for many people in this country." She subsequently received so many death threats that she canceled further speeches. That's what I'm talking about, too.

The world is sinking into deep and violent divides. We need to find stories that help us cross the divides.

Women's Stories

Women are not often placed at the forefront of the Abrahamic faiths, though they are everywhere present. I have been particularly struck by Hagar, Esther, and Mary the mother of

Jesus—their stories on and off the page, how they cross over lines men have made, how they live in and outside of the book.

Hagar starts out in Abraham's Hebrew clan and goes on to become the matriarch of Islam, so the stories go. Esther doesn't live like an observant Jew, but she saves her people from destruction. The official Christian story doesn't exist without Mary, but she also gives birth to so much unorthodox imagination. Her story hums with traces of Indigenous fertility goddesses and ancient Egyptian female deities.

These are some wild and provocative women.

And they keep on living off the page over the centuries, impacting and enlivening human culture from Mecca to Mexico and everywhere in between. Every Muslim man or woman who is physically and financially able is obliged, at least once in life, to follow Hagar, retracing her footsteps during the Hajj, the annual Islamic pilgrimage to Mecca. Jewish girls dress up like Esther every year in Brooklyn, Tel Aviv, and St. Paul— wherever she is celebrated at her festival, Purim. Mary the mother of Jesus shows up in various guises all over the world, inspiring devotion across barriers of religion, class, gender, and race. She is revered by Muslims and Christians and the entirely unorthodox.

> These are some wild and provocative women.

This kind of Girl Power might help us think more creatively about the intersections of Islam, Judaism, and Christianity—as well as about new ways forward that include wisdom, strength, and vulnerability. These women move and live in places and ways that are a little outside the firm foundations and the strict boundaries of our divided traditions. Though our faiths so often follow the guiding visions of the fathers, the women take us different places. They stretch the lines and give the monotheistic faiths a more rambunctious quality.

I've been thinking of Hagar, Esther, and Mary as a sort of transfaith trinity: the (M)other, the Vamp, and the Shape-Shifting Queen. Or sometimes it's the Matriarch on Par with the Patriarch, the Goddess of Love, and the Mediatrix. I don't mean to suggest they are like the Father, the Son, and the Holy Spirit, but I do like invoking a triumvirate.

Following Esther, Hagar, and Mary led me to a Somali mall, where I received a henna tattoo, to a Muslim feminist bookstore, to a temple on Purim, where I met a rabbi dressed as Darth Vader on roller blades, to the feast of Guadalupe, where scantily clad Aztec dancers shook the church foundation in celebration of Our Lady. I encountered many women along the way whose stories, questions, and creative output gave me hope—an artist from Saudi Arabia, a Lutheran convert to Islam, the founder of an Indigenous art and music collective in St. Paul.

Our concept of God is inevitably narrow; it's limited by our experience and the boundaries of our tradition. It helps to get out a little. (I'm embarrassed to admit that getting to know Hagar led me to some of my first theological conversations with Muslim women, conversations where I learned things I hadn't heard before.)

I keep returning to an idea I came across in an essay my friend Abby wrote: "Truth is the sort of thing that is unfinalizable and we would do well to recognize that together we may arrive at more truth than any one of us could alone." Neither heretical nor unobvious, this idea strikes me as a good way to proceed.

Seventeen hundred years ago, Ephrem the Syrian (not exactly your postmodern literary critic) said, "If there were only one meaning for the words of scripture, the first interpreter would find it, and all other listeners would have neither the toil of seeking nor the pleasure of finding."

There is much to find—vast territories to explore, counter-narratives to investigate. God longs for us to participate together in the transformation of the world, but clearly we need to find new routes. The women—ignored and manhandled on occasion, but reliably provocative—have been here all along to help us.

Part One

Abrahamic Faith

1 Go from Your Father's House

Moving to New and Unknown Places

> Only when stability is lost, when given answers no longer offer support, can one reach for a different kind of stability. Stumbling and falling are the means by which standing is achieved.
>
> —Avivah Gottlieb Zornberg

> God made me wander.
>
> —Abraham

Abraham is a strange character. He is considered the Father of Faith, but just look at him. Tries to pass his wife off as his sister. Twice. Sends her to go sleep with other men (to save himself). Leaves one of his sons to die in the desert. Almost murders the other with his bare hands. When he was ninety-nine years old he took a knife and sliced off his own foreskin, saying God told him to do it. Then he does the same to his thirteen-year-old son. Imagine Ishmael's trauma: the old man waving a bloody knife in front of his tender flesh. What kind of faith begins with such a crazy man?

If you look at a map showing the areas of the earth that ascribe to the Abrahamic faiths, you'll discover most of the world defines itself as belonging to one of them. The idea that a group can claim to be the people of God or that a person can say he is the man of God—privileged to know the truth and be blessed over against others—has roots in the Abraham story. This notion has created a lot of violence throughout history. If you were so inclined, you might blame Abraham for 9/11, the Israeli/Palestinian conflict, the Protestant/Catholic wars, the Crusades, Western imperialism, and the systematic extermination of Indigenous culture, language, and religion all over the Americas.

We hear about violence done in the name of religion all the time. Whatever the true forces underlying the violence—politics, poverty, colonialism—much of it has been generated by those who claim to be Abraham's true heirs.

In the twelfth chapter of Genesis, God promises to make Abraham's name great and adds that through Abraham the whole world will be blessed. I guess it depends on how you look at it.

God says to Abraham, "Go from your country and your kindred and your father's house." Leave behind everything you know. God doesn't even say specifically where Abraham is supposed to go—just to the land that God will show him. So he leaves what is fixed and stable to live in a tent. Wanders around with all his stuff dragging behind a camel. Toward what? He doesn't even know what.

Some rabbinical commentaries imagined Abraham as an old man who had lost his mind roaming the desert, mocking voices hounding his consciousness, "look at that foolish, crazy old man wandering aimlessly through the world, looking like a madman." If his progeny have not behaved well toward one another, maybe we could blame it on the instability of the father.

God asks Abraham to leave what he knows for what he will be shown, something he doesn't know yet. It's a lot to ask, really. God says, I give you faith; now follow me—though I am not saying exactly where I'm going, and you don't know that much about me yet. Maybe that's what faith is like.

Some proponents of the Prosperity Gospel look at the passage about God's promised blessing of Abraham, and they say, *name it, claim it*—claim the blessing. I'm not sure what they are thinking.

Abraham was old, and he didn't shave, and he had bad teeth, almost certainly. His wife was old and barren, and she may once have been pretty, but probably not TV-preacher's-wife pretty. His children wouldn't be described as "happy." Isaac and Abraham never speak, in the biblical account, after the scene on Mount Moriah. If God's blessing begins with Abraham's story, it turns out to be a very odd, complicated, and shot-through-with-a-thousand-fragments-of-everything sort of a blessing. *Blessing* is even a weird word to use for what Abraham gets when he starts getting faith.

> *Abraham was old, and he didn't shave, and he had bad teeth, almost certainly. His wife was old and barren, and she may once have been pretty, but probably not TV-preacher's-wife pretty.*

But maybe faith is more like moving than staying put sometimes—trusting in a God who cannot be fully grasped by a religious system. To have faith is to be plunged into the unfathomable. It is, after all, hope in things unseen, as the apostle Paul puts it.

In the midrashim, the rabbis discuss at length why Abraham was chosen. Noah, for instance, is said to be a perfectly righteous man, but the text says nothing about some personal quality that might recommend Abraham to be the father of the faiths (a job that might require some sort of special quality). Avivah Zornberg, a scholar of midrashim, suggests it's his willingness to roam the unknown that qualifies him. He wanders, she says, in the "waste space between clarities." This is the sort of place where grace erupts and "radical astonishment abides."

What does it mean to claim the blessings of Abrahamic faith? It means be unsettled. Abandon safe structures. Suspend what you know in order to discover what you don't know yet. Get lost. Have some vast and hungry questions you don't already know the answers to. That is the energy that moves Abraham from the idolatry of his forbears to intimacy with God.

God promises that Abraham will be generative: "I will make you exceedingly fruitful." His descendants will outnumber the stars. And although it seems doubtful for a time, he and the women with whom he sojourns really do end up generating a lot. Think of all the offspring these parents of the faith have generated: Isaac and Ishmael, David and Solomon, Jehoshaphat, Muhammad and Jesus. Rumi, Rabia, Rashi, Oscar Romero, the Southern Baptists, St. Theresa, Joan of Arc, Luther and Barth, the pope, monks and libertines. It's a little out of control—all this fruit, a vast and complicated blessing.

God doesn't give Abraham rules or obligations—a particular system he is supposed to use to create a religion. (That all comes later.) God tells Abraham to begin the journey to a land he will be shown. There's a sense that the land is good, but the land is a lot more than simply flowing with milk and honey. There are foreigners. There are famines. The land is full of *others*, this land where faith leads. Claim the blessings of faith. It's a little uncomfortable, perhaps, but not unexciting. Maybe to be a true heir of Abraham you just need to be willing to go on a journey. You don't have to travel far to discover things you don't know—like a fruit you've never tasted or a word you've never heard.

In a drawn-out scene near the end of Abraham's story, he tries to buy some land to bury his wife Sarah. As he's haggling with the owners of the land, he says, "I am just an alien and a sojourner among you." (A sojourner still! He's like 175!) He doesn't settle down until he himself is buried on this little piece of ground he acquires from a foreigner—the only bit of the Promised Land he ever actually comes to possess.

But the text says that Abraham died old and contented—in a ripe age. Ripe. How do you get to be that—fully grown and tender, full of complexity and sweetness? Maybe by roaming around awhile in the waste space between clarities, maybe by doing that a lot.

The branches of Abraham's family—Jews, Christians, Muslims (and actually Baha'i, Druze, and Rastafarians, too)—have followed paths that, for the most part, have been laid down by men, but it would certainly be in the spirit of *Abrahamic* faith to leave the well-worn paths—to sojourn beyond the familiar, to spend time wandering among women.

2 Rambunctious Monotheism
The Feminine Face of God

This I think is worth attending to: the "mono" in monotheism can have at least two valences. One of them is
restrictive, zealously hygienic let us say, because God is
in rivalry with other gods and needs everything to be
narrowed down and made more exact, since the danger
of idolatry is everywhere. The other is not in rivalry with
anything at all, and is seriously concerned that we will
not have enough joy and freedom and happiness unless
we are set free from our fear of death and enabled to dare
to participate in the life of the Creator. And the more
signs of our being loved and encouraged and enabled to
belong we get, the merrier. It is this rumbustiousness of
God whose monotheism is decidedly unhygienic, whose
oneness is nothing at all like our monisms, trying to get
through to us that we are loved.

—James Alison,
"Living the Magnificat with Rossini and Mary"

Every day when I come to work in my office above the garage,
I look at the poster above my desk. It says, "Monotheism
without contemplation is dangerous." It is an advertisement
for a series of talks James Alison, the Catholic priest and

theologian, gave at House of Mercy. We had an artist make a likeness of Alison where he looks like James Bond. We listed a website at the bottom, dangerism.com, which doesn't exist (at least not the last time I checked). I can't remember what we were thinking. It was a long time ago. But the poster has an enduring impact on me. Not because Alison looks so dapper, but because monotheism without contemplation *is* dangerous.

Not that the violence monotheism has wrought is hard to keep in mind. The media is full of references to "Islamic extremism." History is strewn with terrible moments of "Christian extremism." The Bible is even full of this violence—the conquest of Canaan, the destruction brought about by kings. Josiah "hewed down" the temples of Baal and Asherah and burned the bones of their priests. The violence in the Bible is often about purging the land of idolatry. But one might ask if idolatry is being destroyed or advanced with all that vengeful passion.

Gender and number were relatively unimportant at the inception of the faith of Israel. One male God was not above all others. The Queen of Heaven, for example, was likely seen as Yahweh's female consort. We hear about her from Jeremiah's objections to her. She was probably a part of what the people of Israel had come to worship. You can see traces of the feminine face of God throughout the text. God is imaged as a mother bear, a mother eagle, a woman who gives birth, a nursing mother, a midwife. *El Shaddai*, usually translated "Almighty God," can also be translated "Breasted One."

The beloved mother, the companion to women giving birth—sometimes known as Asherah, or the consort of El, or the mother of all living—was popular among the people.

179

Archeologists have not found evidence for the Exodus, or Joshua's conquest, or for many of the events recorded in the Hebrew Scriptures, but they have found thousands of little Asherah figurines buried in the dirt—amidst the rubble of kitchens, and bedrooms, and playgrounds, and shrines—all over the Holy Land.

The people who wrote down and edited the stories about the history of Israel were hoping to strengthen an emerging monotheism. They attempted to do this in part by getting rid of the mother. I keep imagining (and I admit my imagination may not be historically accurate) the people of Israel—all these rural sheep-farmers, goat-herders, and moms with their babies who live all over the countryside. They are preliterate. They work their gardens, tend their sheep, and sometimes pray to the rain god for rain. When the women are in labor they clutch their female figurines. Maybe they have some little shrines in their backyards where they practice a sort of piety that they have always practiced: they burn incense to "idols"—a sort of religion that almost all people everywhere had practiced—comfortable with various gods, mixed gods. But the kings in Kings are judged bad or good according to one criterion: Did they keep the people from burning incense to idols?

Once Israel had been defeated and exiled by Babylon, the enormous empire of the day, editors revised the history to show that bad things happened to Israel because the people were unfaithful to Yahweh. It was because people worshipped other gods.

Of course they did. Monotheism had hardly been established—had barely taken hold—before the exile. These editors may have been doing something important to help build the faith of the community in exile. And it is true, I believe, that we suffer when we fail to trust God. The Hebrew Bible portrays this existential struggle with beauty and grace but it also seems true to me, standing here in the twenty-first century, that we could have benefitted from a few more glimpses of the God who labors, the midwife God, the mother God, the breasted one.

It didn't take long, once my daughter, Olivia, started choosing her own books for our shelves, to fill them with every YA novel that included Greek, Norse, or Egyptian mythology. When she crawled into bed with me at night, she was all Artemis this, Athena that—did I know about the Valkyrie? She Elephants? Isis? Fine—she was into goddesses, but I wished there were more stories from our tradition that could satisfy her yearning for the feminine face of the divine. I know it's there in the Bible. We don't believe God is male, after all. It just takes some work to uncover these images in Abrahamic monotheism—they have been buried.

Alison's poster quote, "Monotheism without contemplation is dangerous," comes from an essay he wrote for a festival celebrating Julian of Norwich in which he also says, "Monotheism is a terrible idea, but a wonderful discovery." As an idea it seems to get us riled up against other ideas—defining ourselves and our people over against other selves and other people.

The books of 1 and 2 Kings describe one evil queen who must be defeated if the people of God are to survive: Jezebel. Though the gods Jezebel worships (the gods of plants and trees, as the Arch Books children's series puts it) seem less destructive than our gods of capital and ideology, she is intensely vilified and meets a vividly depicted, violent death.

She is trampled by horses and her body is devoured by dogs, except (the text says) for "the skull, and the feet, and the palms of her hands." In a chillingly brutal scene, the female queen with the power in the castle, who worships a female deity with power in the temple, becomes dog food.

It's no wonder it's taken centuries to start reclaiming some feminine imagery.

Learning to Trust God

"Monotheism is a terrible idea but a wonderful discovery." The quest for monotheistic purity leads to violence. The contemplation that might lead away from it involves a self-critical listening, says Alison. And we do see this sort of self-criticism emerge all over the Hebrew text. Self-criticism allows us to see our similarity to our neighbor. We, like the rest of humanity— all our brothers and sisters and cousins and aunts, Taoists, Rastafarians, Muslims, Zoroastrians, Hindus, and Jews, are people in the process of being transformed by the grace of God. We are learning to trust this God, but we aren't there yet.

Learning to trust this God who is not opposed to other gods, or different truths, or strange people, but rather who longs to gather all things to her bosom happens over time in a relationship. It isn't an idea we embrace or reject; it is a relationship we are in.

When we encounter monotheism as an idea, we get hung up on the numerical data. One is a number. As a number it is rather like other numbers—different in quantity but not quality from seventeen. It might be helpful, Alison suggests, to think less of the number one and more of the expression God "is."

The Bible has a lively abundance—an unruly surplus of metaphors—when it tries to speak of God. God is unique, hard to describe, impossible to contain. But in order to speak of God, in order to communicate, we point widely and wildly.

Taking the "Mono-" out of *Monotheism*

The "mono-" in *monotheism* isn't entirely helpful. That syllable gets us thinking in terms of monolith, monoculture, monopoly. A monocarpic plant is a plant that flowers and bears fruit only once. A monolith is massive, solid, and uniform. Monostylous means having only one style. You get where I'm going.

The Bible has a lively abundance—an unruly surplus of metaphors— when it tries to speak of God. God is unique, hard to describe, impossible to contain.

The Union of Concerned Scientists says monoculture (cultivating a single type of plant to increase yield and profit) reduces biodiversity and is destroying our planet. Perhaps "mono-" doesn't suggest what we'd hope when we talk about God.

The Trinity (though arrived at as a doctrine rather laboriously and, some might say, artificially) is a beautiful alternative metaphor. God is "essentially relational, ecstatic, fecund, alive as passionate love," as Catherine LaCugna puts it. Of course, Christians have also used the Trinity to talk about God as an angry father taking out his rage on his son to free us from the terrible wrath. Although it can be a beautiful metaphor, it isn't always.

Christian, Muslim, and Jewish theologians have spent a lot of time coming up with the best metaphors for God that they can imagine. Islam rejects the Trinity. If people who practice Islam view the Trinity as "self-indulgent guess work about things nobody can possibly know or prove" (as Karen Armstrong puts it), I can understand that. I can even see some merit in it. Perhaps we do experience God more as an epiphany than as a doctrine, as Islam would have it.

We have tried hard to focus our attention on God throughout history, to come up with the best metaphors we can imagine. But the sort of truth we find with faith is unfinalizable—because it is more like love than math.

The proliferation of metaphors we find in the Bible might lead us to believe God is more like many things than one thing: God is a lily, a rose, dew, wind, and fire. God is a mother bear and a lion. God is not in the fire or the wind but in a still small voice.

We don't know exactly what we're talking about when we talk about God. Some mystics determined it was better to remain silent in the face of the mystery. Apophatic theology suggests the best we can do is to say what we know God is not. We need more silence. It also helps to get out and look around—to listen to what other people (our cousins and neighbors) are thinking. If we need help seeing something new (or seeing something old in a new way), we might start by listening to the women and reclaiming the feminine face of the Abrahamic faiths.

Despite the Overwhelming Maleness

Even though our Scripture may be patriarchal materials mostly handed down, interpreted, and performed by men over hundreds of years, the search for God in our midst is not over. We're not done yet. God's not done yet.

Yes, the male metaphors and the male characters in the stories of the Bible often get more sustained attention. Yes, Yahweh comes across as pretty "male." "His" leading prophets are male: Abraham, Moses, Isaiah, Jeremiah, Ezekiel, Daniel—all male. Jesus is male. As are Peter, and John, and Matthew, Mark, Luke, and Paul. Around two hundred women are named in the Bible and 1,181 men.

But despite all this overwhelming maleness, here's what starts to happen when the women show up: things shift.

Most women in the Bible are actually a little out there—not at all like June Cleaver, or the Model Evangelical Women of the seventies, or whatever version of the virtuous woman churches peddled in your youth. My sister and I remember a special Sunday school class for "young ladies" where we studied Proverbs 31 to learn what it means to be a good woman. She "eateth not the bread of idleness." She "riseth also while it is yet night, and giveth meat to her household." The good woman, according to our teacher, was primarily someone who was obedient to her husband. I'm sure the curriculum was generated, in part, by the fear that disobedient women would disrupt the status quo—after all, we were just past the rebellions of the sixties. A lot of people weren't into the status quo.

The women in the Bible generally don't conform to the image of the virtuous woman I learned in Sunday school. They don't look like good evangelicals. Or like the medieval Christian saints—women who, according to the men who wrote about them, were not interested in food, sex, or pleasure of any kind. The hagiographers (usually men) praised female saints for such amazing holy feats as eating nothing for three years or being miraculously free from excreting. Columba of Rieti, according to some reports, "excreted neither feces nor urine, did not menstruate, never sweated except from the armpits, discharged no filth or dandruff from her hair, and only occasionally gave forth spittle from her mouth or tears from her eyes."

Hagar weeps. Esther pleases her pagan king sexually. Mary gives birth.

Saint Ida of Louvain, so the stories go, ate only moldy bread—she didn't want anything to pass her lips that tasted pleasant. Once she went for eleven days eating only the little flowers of the lime tree. In contrast to all this extraordinary asceticism, Mary, Martha's sister, washes Jesus feet to excess with a pound (a pound!) of scented oil and wipes his feet with her hair.

Traditional interpretations often read the anointing woman in the gospels as subservient, but I can tell you she was not following any rules for proper behavior. She's brazenly sensual. She violated hefty, enduring, societal norms. The women in the Bible are generally not very saint-like, honestly, and yet they are often flattened out to fit into the role of moral examples. You come across this in feminist readings as well: Are the women strong? Ethical? Are they good examples for women to follow? I'm not sure that's a helpful way to read. Scripture reveals who we are and who God is. It ushers us into a relationship more than providing examples for us to follow.

That said, women in the Bible are more subversive than subservient. Rather than fit seamlessly into the patriarchal narratives, they disrupt them.

Hagar is blessed in the same way Abraham is: giving birth to a whole people—a whole other faith, as it turns out. Esther saves her people not through being pure or virginal—quite the opposite. Mary the mother of Jesus is, well, the mother of God. To say these stories are edgy is to minimize them. They undermine the dominant patriarchal narrative in significant ways.

These women's stories were often an embarrassment to the church fathers—stories of human people who had sex, and children, and unseemly emotions. The church fathers argued a lot about how to understand these old stories, clean them up, make them edifying. Our readings are still distorted by their effort.

> *Women in the Bible are more subversive than subservient. Rather than fit seamlessly into the patriarchal narratives, they disrupt them.*

But you can't really cover up the women's inappropriate behavior. A woman with her hair and her pound of perfume remains.

Not long after Mary, Martha's sister, anoints Jesus with the perfume and her hair, Jesus does something similar for his disciples (almost as though he took a cue from her). He lays aside his garments, wraps a towel around his waist, pours water into a basin, and begins to wash the disciples' feet—wiping their feet with the towel that he was using to cover himself. Almost as intimate as if he had used his hair. That's a crazy story to illustrate the love of God. Talk about disarming love! It subverts the usual power paradigm.

We need these stories about a God who gives up power for love. You can have an *Abrahamic* and *monotheistic* faith that is not determined by the power of the patriarchy.

God is not sitting on a throne our systems built. God is much more lively than static, more rambunctious than monotonous. Behind the "mono-" is a mother/father/lover—a riotous garden with many blooms, not a monoculture. Whatever God "is" has been described by Sufi mystics here, Pseudo-Dionysius there, Luther, Hildegard, Thérèsè, Bridget, Karl Barth here and there. No one with any respect for the enterprise claims to have yet nailed it. And all agree that we need to keep tilling the soil.

Part Two

Hagar

3 The Biblical Story
A Matriarch on Par with a Patriarch

Your task is not to seek for love, but merely to seek and
find all the barriers within yourself that you have built
against it.

—Jalal ad-Din Rumi

Any good poem, any good human being, any good story
spins against the way it drives.

—David Milch

Pictures of penguins, chickens, and goats in sweaters, a
baby hedgehog wearing miniscule red booties someone
apparently made by hand—I keep clicking on these slide-
shows in my Facebook feed (I spent fifteen minutes wading
through adds to see what the *Little House on the Prairie* cast
looks like now), along with the cat videos. I'm not proud
of this but I can't seem to help myself. Some part of me is
driven to distraction. I need something to break up the
bad news. At first it seems surreal: "Government Agencies
Forbidden from Speaking to Press," "The Word 'Science'
Disappears from Environmental Protection Agency." Then
it becomes infuriating: "Immigrant Children Separated
from Parents at the Border." So I sign four or ten petitions

(which seems like an impotent gesture). Then I swear to God I will stay off the Internet forever, which lasts two days.

But then in other stories you can see so much creative energy exploding. A collection of women artists launches "The Other Border Wall Project." They receive designs for a pipe organ wall, a drinkable wall, and a wall of hammocks (among others). Over one hundred thousand people showing up for the Women's March in St. Paul when planners expected twenty thousand. And the National Park Rangers going rogue—with the "Unofficial Resistance Team of the US National Park Service."

I have loved the National Park Rangers' amphitheater fireside talks my whole life, with all their intricate knowledge of verdant forests and subalpine habitat, the pitch and tempo of the white-throated sparrow's song. But I never saw them as leaders of the resistance—rogue rangers for mercy.

We need the Good News. We need a story about a God acting against overwhelming forces of injustice, a God who doesn't side with power. The story of Hagar is one of those stories—one where God makes a way out of no way.

We get quite a few stories like this in the Bible. The Hebrew Scripture often embodies the spirit of subversion. It barely lays down its dominant narrative before it starts to undermine the tyranny of a singular, over-simplified narrative. It doesn't suppress the possibility of opposing narratives. It plants the seed for them.

Is this the way the word of God works? Setting our imaginations free to be graceful—free from the inevitability of submission to power?

The Bible is not good propaganda. Its "heroes" lie, steal, and drink too much. It establishes institutions (priesthood, temple, church) and then undermines them by counternarratives that expose their corruption. Stories are told and then revised; the people of God are condemned and redeemed. The Bible is not a slick promotional tool for a nation, or an institution, or even a particular set of beliefs. It's a witness to a God who is profoundly alive. This is a beautiful thing about monotheism: it keeps renouncing idolatry in favor of a lover who resists calculation, a lover who knows no bounds.

The Hebrew Bible often comes across as undermining its own plot. Like there's a story it's trying to tell, but it keeps interrupting itself, as if some prophet followed the official storytellers around—yelling out obfuscations to muddle the dominant narrative. It spins against the way it drives.

At the glorious moment of the Exodus, when the Israelites are about to be delivered from slavery, the story suddenly zeros in on the houses of the Egyptians where, we are told, you could hear a terrible crying "such as there has never been, nor ever shall be again." All the Egyptian families who have lost children to the final plague are weeping. Readers get a sense of righteous justice when the slave master Pharaoh is punished, but the text continues to the point where you can't really keep that feeling going. Not only is the first born of Pharaoh struck by the plague, but the first born of the maidservant, the first born of the captive, the first born of the cattle—you start to feel for the enemy.

The people have been enslaved in Egypt by a powerful Pharaoh, but it was Joseph, one of their own, who put into motion their enslavement. The Pharaoh is cruel, oppresses the people, won't let them go—but it is God, the text says repeatedly, who hardens Pharaoh's heart. The questions stand up, walk around, slap you in the face. God hardened Pharaoh's heart? Really? Why? Did the maidservant have to lose her child?

The word of God is a revelation meant to bind us to each other and God—not to enforce enemy lines.

People often read the stories as if they were meant to create a sense of "us" and "them," but that way of reading misses the pulsing, merciful heart of Scripture. The word of God is a revelation meant to bind us to each other and God—not to enforce enemy lines.

A Woman Demeaned

The way some of us heard it told in Sunday school, the story of Hagar and Ishmael predicted inevitable animosity among the branches of Abraham's family, explaining the perpetual strife between the Arabs and the Jewish people over the land of Israel. In the Sunday school telling, this story about a mother and her son and the tender love of God justified a sort of hopelessness, a boundary. We should try reading it differently.

Paul isn't exactly helpful in this regard. He offers a convoluted argument that Hagar and Ishmael are enemies of freedom. His reading of the story is creative, if strained and bizarre. Paul makes Hagar into an object of scorn. He takes up Sarah's cruel words in the story as if they were God's command "Cast out the slave (that enemy of freedom) and her child." Islam wasn't yet on the scene, but his argument is used by its detractors when it does come along.

Martin Luther ups the antagonism—accuses Hagar of kidnapping Abraham's son. And claims she's the cause of all the sins of the family. Calvin disparages Hagar for having a wild and intractable temper. Although this doesn't seem quite fair, it's not surprising. Women have to field similar accusations all the time for raising their voices or standing for their rights.

I don't remember exactly how my Baptist Sunday school spun the story, but I came away with the impression that Hagar was seductive or sultry—the archetypal other woman. I learned Abraham's relationship with Hagar was a mistake. Isaac, Abraham's son through Sarah, was sweet and compliant, but Ishmael, Hagar's son, was gruff and insolent. This was likely conveyed with a narrow-eyed or suspicious-looking flannel board character. The upshot: Ishmael "mocked" his half-brother and deserved to be banished by God to the desert.

That lesson might help some parents curb sibling rivalry, but I never banished one of my children to the desert, so I can't say for sure. The lesson hangs on one Hebrew word, *m'tzahek*, that can be translated as "mocked," as well as in many non-sinister ways, like *playing* or *laughing*. The text is anything but clear on the moral qualities of the characters involved. That doesn't seem to be the point of the story.

For a woman whom God clearly hears, helps, and sees, readers have spent a lot of energy diminishing Hagar. Her story undermines the official patriarchal narrative, so perhaps it's not surprising she's been demeaned.

The grand narrative in Genesis is about Israel. It's about Abraham's heirs through Isaac—and God's blessing of the Jewish people. Hagar's story thrusts out in an entirely different direction, with Abraham's other son and the other woman.

Hagar's name means *other, outsider, stranger*. Who let her in?

Resilience and Resistance

For a female protagonist in the Bible, Hagar has a remarkable story. Two fairly long, detailed passages are given to Hagar in Genesis, even though these narratives disrupt the patriarchal plot lines.

Though Hagar didn't receive much positive attention in the white church I grew up in, the African American church has long recognized the importance of her place in Scripture. In *Sisters in the Wilderness*, the landmark work that helped establish African American womanist theology, Delores Williams says, "For more than a hundred years Hagar—the African slave of the Hebrew woman Sarah—has appeared in the deposits of African-American culture. Sculptors, writers, poets, scholars, preachers and just plain folks have passed along the biblical figure Hagar to generation after generation of black folks." Reading the story from Hagar's point of view, these African American communities see her as the central character instead of Sarah or Abraham. Hagar's heritage was African. She was a black woman and a slave—brutalized by the slaveholder, Sarah.

> *Hagar's name means other, outsider, stranger. Who let her in?*

In the narrative, God's voice first enters in conversation with Hagar, not her oppressors (something Paul the apostle didn't seem to regard). "Hagar becomes the first female in the Bible to liberate herself from oppressive power structures," writes Williams. That is no enemy of freedom.

Hagar emerges as a resilient mother in Williams's rereading and an important figure of female resistance among many African American communities.

The God Who Sees

Here's the basic narrative: Sarah, Abraham's wife, can't get pregnant. She knows that Abraham needs an heir, so she tells him to have sex with her Egyptian maid. Hagar gets pregnant. Sarah (theoretically) should be happy, but she isn't. Most translations say that once Hagar got pregnant, she looked at Sarah with "contempt," but the Hebrew is actually softer than that—something more along the lines of "Hagar looked at Sarah with less esteem." Maybe that was because Sarah forced her to have sex with her eighty-five-year-old husband. Maybe it was because Sarah was asking her to bear a child she would have to give away. There are many reasons Hagar might have looked at Sarah with less esteem.

Sarah tells Abraham that she doesn't like the way Hagar looked at her. Likely insecure, menopausal, definitely beyond child-bearing years, perhaps Sarah's prone to irritable misinterpretation. She wanted to be the one carrying the baby. But however Hagar was looking at Sarah, it's hardly evidence that Hagar had a wild and intractable temper.

In the text Abraham seems to empathize with Sarah. He tells her to do what she wants with Hagar. When Sarah deals "harshly with her," Hagar flees. She escapes to the wilderness in the same way the Israelites will later flee their slavery and go into the wilderness. The text uses the same word to describe Sarah's harsh treatment of Hagar as it will later use to describe the Egyptian Pharaoh's treatment of the Israelites. Here a Hebrew oppresses an Egyptian. Later in the narrative this will be reversed. As Israel's moral codes develop, how the community treats the outsider becomes a crucial component of the law of Israel: "you must not mistreat or oppress" her. But Sarah beats the other, and Hagar runs away.

Sarah is the official founding matriarch; she's the one who supposedly births the legitimate heir—but it's not clear if you can trust her. At this point in the story, our sympathy is drawn toward the outsider. I respect that in a founding narrative. The story of the chosen people includes the other deep in the heart of it.

Out in the wilderness alone, Hagar's chances for survival aren't high. But an angel of the Lord finds her in the desert. Hagar is the first person in Scripture to receive such a messenger. The angel tells her to go back to camp because, "Behold, you are with child, and shall bear a son: you shall call his name Ishmael." This is not the only time we hear such a line in the Bible, but it is the first biblical annunciation. An angel will say these same words to Mary, the mother of Jesus.

Through the angel, God gives Hagar, this woman—the other, the Egyptian outsider, the non-Hebrew—the same promise God gave Abraham, the patriarch—saying, "I will so greatly multiply your descendants that they cannot be numbered for multitude."

And then Hagar—the only person in the Bible to do this—gives God a name. A woman names God. What thrilling audacity! She calls God "The God Who Sees"—a beautiful name. This God pays attention to her and draws near enough to see her. Hagar's God is not a narcissistic deity obsessed with being seen—this God sees her—sees her suffering. This God finds her in the desert and helps her.

The Wild Ass

The angel says Ishmael will be "a wild ass of a man." To contemporary readers this may sound insulting. But in the Bible, the wild ass is most notably free. In Job, God speaks adoringly of the animal, who hears not the shouts of the driver, ranges the mountain as his pasture, and searches after every green thing (a type of rogue ranger). Maybe this is the angel's reassurance that, in spite of the fact the she is instructed to go back to camp, Hagar and her son won't live their lives enslaved to the powers.

Hagar is an outlier, an Egyptian, and though Sarah deals with her harshly, God is tender with her, watches over her, intervenes for her protection, and promises her that she will be the mother of a great nation. And Hagar does go back to camp to give birth to her son—which was probably a good move for their survival.

Eventually Sarah miraculously gets pregnant when Abraham was one hundred years old. Her son Isaac is the "true" heir. On the day Isaac is weaned, Abraham throws a big party. Maybe Sarah's been drinking because she couldn't drink while she was nursing (and maybe this is why you have a festival of weaning). Maybe she's a mean drunk, but she sees Ishmael "playing" with Isaac at this party (this is the word that can be translated many ways). Upset, she decides that Hagar and Ishmael should be sent to the wilderness to die.

There's a lot of midrash—rabbinic commentary—in the ancient Talmud on this text. The rabbis asked a lot of questions about it—and it invites a lot of questions. Sarah wants to send a boy and his mother to their deaths. Some interpreters defend Sarah. They say Sarah was an incisive judge of humanity and knew that the two sons of Abraham could never live peacefully together. Abraham, on the other hand, was too entangled with the other—letting complexity get in the way of clarity. Sarah makes it clear: "The son of this slave woman shall not be heir with my son."

Soon we meet a heart-wrenching scene. Abraham doesn't want to send the boy and his mother away. The day they are to depart, Abraham gets up early, takes some food and a skin of water, and puts them on Hagar's shoulder. When the water is gone, Hagar places her dying child under a bush and sits down and pleads, "Please don't make me watch my boy die." Again, a first. This is the most emotion we've seen displayed in the Bible so far. Hagar is the first person in the Bible to weep. Hagar reaches out emotionally to the God who sees and God sees her. God tells her not to be afraid. "Lift up the lad and hold him fast with your hand; for I will make of him a great nation."

In the narrative of Genesis you don't see God acting quite so mercifully and tenderly in response to humans until you see God with Hagar. This is not a mighty warrior god or a distant impassive creator. God disrupts the official patriarchal plot here. It's as though the story knows what it wants to tell:

Isaac is the chosen one, the Israelites are the chosen people, but then another brightly intense other narrative drops. Hagar and Ishmael not only survive in the wilderness; they thrive.

There's a small line at the end of the story. You might not even notice it's there or think it's important: Hagar finds a wife for her son. This is the only time in the Bible where a woman finds a wife for her son. Men find wives for their boys. It's a patriarchy: you don't let a woman mess with the lines.

Hagar is the first person in the Bible to weep. Hagar reaches out emotionally to the God who sees and God sees her. God tells her not to be afraid.

Hagar messes with the lines.

To a remarkable degree, Hagar's story parallels Abraham's. She takes the first son into the wilderness, where his death seems imminent until an angel speaks and shows her a well. Abraham takes the second son up to Mount Moriah, where his death seems imminent until an angel speaks and shows him a ram. Even the language in the two incidents is parallel, occasionally using the same words.

Abraham is the central character in the Isaac story. Hagar is the central character in the Ishmael story. Here, from the beginnings of Scripture, is a matriarch on par with the patriarch.

Though the narrative diverges to follow Abraham and Isaac, the Hebrew text lets this woman, the blessed other, stand in its history—like a beautiful question. God blesses an Egyptian matriarch in the midst of an ironclad Hebrew patriarchy.

No matter how the dominant narrative is inclined, the Hagar story planted in the middle of it is also planting the question, What if the narrative had followed the mother?

Love, Not Sacrifice

In the chapter immediately following the tender story of Hagar and Ishmael, the story of God takes a sudden shift: God comes across as callous—almost cruel. God, so the story goes, asks Abraham to "Take your son, your only son, whom you love, and go to the land of Moriah, and offer him there as a burnt offering." God asks Abraham to kill his son. Abraham doesn't argue with God as he quietly gets up in the morning, gathers his son, saddles his ass, and trudges up the mountain.

Think about these two parents who are placed side by side. Hagar weeps when she sees her child might die. Abraham agrees without question to do what God commands, even if it means killing his child. For this he is seen as a devout example of what it means to have faith. All of the Abrahamic faiths have found inspiration in this story of Abraham's willingness to murder his son. It doesn't take a lot of imagination to understand that we might want to rethink that.

How is it that we fail to pay much attention to the story where the protagonist and God are emotionally engaged over the fate of a child and shift all our attention to the story of the male parent?

The story of the near-sacrifice of Isaac is never mentioned again in the Hebrew Scripture, unlike the Exodus, for example, which is remembered over and over again. Clearly the psalmist, the prophets, and the poets did not take it up as a shining example of who God is and what faith looks like. The story starts receiving more attention at the end of the first millennium BCE, when the Israelites face persecution. Abraham's act becomes an important symbol for the type of sacrifice pious individuals must be willing to make. But "are you willing to kill for your God?" is not a question that has led to good places.

Holding up the story of the patriarch alone here makes it seem like God pits parental love against great faith. While this opposition does end up being emphasized in the history of the patriarchal religious system, I'm not sure that's what God had in mind. Look at God with Hagar.

In a book that explores the Abrahamic faiths, Bruce Feiler writes, "this willingness to make the 'ultimate sacrifice' for God is the most troubling legacy of Abraham's life. Abraham is not just a gentle man of peace, but a model for fanaticism as much as moderation. . . . He nurtured in his very behavior . . . the intimate connection between faith and violence. And then by elevating such conduct to the standard of piety, he stirred in his descendants a similar desire to lash out, to view pain as an arm of belief, and to use brutality to advance their vision of a divine centered world."

Maybe we've been focusing on the wrong story. Look at the mother, because her story is here, too—the matriarch on par with the patriarch. Far from doing violence or being willing to do violence, Hagar challenges God to help her child live.

The patriarch is supposed to show his love for God by being willing to kill his child, a distorted challenge and the ultimate exercise in emotional detachment. Abraham, according to a liturgical prayer, "suppressed his compassion in order to perform thy will with a perfect heart." Not like I know everything, but is that how it works? God is alive as passionate love. God longs to draw us into God's merciful compassion—not separate us from our feeling.

Maybe Abraham's story was never meant to be exemplary. It's more of a narrative about what moving from idolatry to faith in a living, universal, loving, merciful God looks like. Mistakes are inevitably made along the way. The old gods required sacrifice. The God who sustains all beings, loves all things—birds and water and sheep and goats—doesn't want your sacrifice, but rather your love.

Hagar's story isn't grandiose. What makes her inspiring isn't some singular heroic zeal, but something we all have access to in an almost daily way: love. And it's not some sort of noble, abstract, rarified love—it's very human. She cries to God to save someone she loves. This is Hagar's faith—she sees her child thirsty and she longs to fill his thirst. She isn't asked to detach from her feeling to prove her faith. Faith is something as close to her, and as natural to her, as her own breath. What if faith is something like that instead of something we have to strive for—something more like breathing than striving for purity?

> *Maybe we've been focusing on the wrong story. Look at the mother, because her story is here, too—the matriarch on par with the patriarch. Hagar challenges God to help her child live.*

Near the end of Abraham's life, after Sarah has died, Abraham marries Keturah. According to midrashic tradition, Keturah is actually Hagar's real name. Hagar was just a descriptive name, meaning *other*, but Keturah was her real name. Far from cutting off the counter-narrative, Abraham embraces it. Takes it into his heart. Lays in bed with it—makes love with Hagar again and they have many more children. In this reading the world is not hopelessly divided. There isn't one side or the other. Hagar and Abraham embrace in their old age. Boundaries are blurred. God's love is let loose. May this somehow be so.

4 The Mother of Islam
Looking for Hagar in the Qur'an,
a Tattoo Parlor, and an Art Gallery

Suppose we admitted for the sake of argument that
motherhood was powerful.
—Laurel Thatcher Ulrich

Transcend literally means . . . to cross over, to bridge, or
to make connections. A truly transcendent God knows
the bounds of no human life or location but is always
too actively crossing over boundaries to become any
group's source of special privilege. We have "stuck God"
with a notion of transcendence that is a projection of
those who are used to being in charge.
—Karen Bloomquist

There's a little mention in 1 Chronicles 5:18–22 of the Reubenites defeating the Hagarites in battle. The Reubenites take
50,000 camels and 250,000 sheep from the Hagarites. Some
scholars say the tribe wasn't related to Hagar; others disagree.
The twelve tribes of Israel were all named after men, naturally.

But what if Hagar's matriarchal clan flourished out there
in the desert? Maybe the loss of camels and sheep didn't even
concern her—they still had their goats, and goat milk, and
herb-encrusted goat cheese. Or maybe they were more into

plant-based diets anyway and felt relieved to see some of the animal products leave.

The Hebrew Scripture plants this potentially subversive seed: the blessed Other/Mother—or (M)Other—and leaves it. But it doesn't simply wither and die. While the Hebrew Scripture has few stories about Hagar and Ishmael, the Islamic tradition has many. Christianity and Judaism may have maligned her, but in Islam, Hagar is the matriarch of monotheism. It is through Ishmael that Muhammad eventually arrives. In Islamic tradition God leads Hagar into the wilderness so that through her a new faith might be born—a faith that allows a whole lot of "others" to encounter Abraham's God.

The Islamic stories are similar to the ones in the Hebrew Scripture. Hagar and Ishmael are sent to the wilderness, where they run out of water. Determined to save her son, Hagar starts running back and forth between two hills, trying to get up high enough to spot a caravan that might help her. After her seventh run, Ishmael kicks the ground with his heel and a miraculous well springs out of the ground. It's called the Zamzam well. When Muslims make their journey to Mecca, it's part of their pilgrimage to reenact Hagar's maternal determination by running seven times between the hills. Then they drink from the Zamzam, and they take some of the water back home in memory of Hagar.

The Ka'aba, located in Mecca, is the holiest shrine in Islam. According to Islamic tradition, it was first built by Adam and then rebuilt later by Abraham and Ishmael when Abraham came to visit his son. When Abraham leaves Hagar and Ishmael in the wilderness, he leaves them at the Ka'aba site, "The House of God." In the Hebrew Scripture Abraham seems to abandon Ishmael, but in the Islamic stories he keeps coming back to visit this side of his family. These are heartbreaking and beautiful stories. One son in one place, one in the other—Abe trudging back and forth, the father of not one, but two faiths. Abraham loves both of his wives and both of his sons.

Meeting My Muslim Neighbor

I live on a farm in rural Minnesota, just east of a town called Milaca. I don't actually have any Muslim neighbors. We were looking for affordable property with some pretty features when our little community of friends decided to settle here. We didn't have children yet. We didn't think of all the implications. The Mille Lacs Indian Reservation is an hour north of us. St. Cloud, with a large Somali population, is an hour west. But Milaca is 95 percent white and mostly evangelical with a few Lutherans and Catholics thrown in—64.4 percent of the residents voted for Trump in the last presidential election, 28.6 percent voted for Clinton. We have one of the most renowned lutefisk suppers in the state: the largest "cross-cultural" event is Swedish.

Central Minnesota is a popular destination for traveling speakers whose main objective is to spread fear about Islam. A former FBI agent who left the agency amidst some scandal has built a new career spreading alarm in our part of the state. He asks the crowds who come to see him if they are prepared to deal with dozens of jihadists with mortars and shoulder-fired rockets. He says Muslims are buying up gas stations and working at airports to pave the way for a violent takeover. Another speaker, the son of a Baptist preacher, who spoke at more than twenty events in central Minnesota in a year and a half, tells his audience that Islam is not a religion. It is a savage cult. He argues for the mass deportation of Muslims from the United States. Minnesota Public Radio reported that an audience member at one of these talks reasoned that people who don't actually have Muslim neighbors are better suited to assess Islam's threat because "if you're rubbing shoulders with a lot of Muslims," you might be persuaded to believe they are not so menacing.

I Decide to Take a Different Approach

I wanted to rub shoulders with as many Muslim women as possible. I wanted to hear from them about Hagar. Since that wasn't likely to happen in my neighborhood, I started contacting every mosque and Islamic organization I could find in a seventy-five mile radius. I wouldn't be surprised if I am now on some government surveillance list. I worried a little that if I followed Hagar into her Islamic terrain, I might be disappointed by all the patriarchy I'd find there. I am so weary of finding it in my own tradition, I wasn't sure I could handle it in another. One way to avoid it, I decided, was to gather the stories of women.

Henna Tattoos at the Somali Mall

When I ask Angel, a friend of mine, if she can help me meet Muslim women, she suggests we go to the Somali mall in Minneapolis to get henna tattoos. Angel is a teacher who works with immigrants. Like an angel, she is ever attentive to whoever is vulnerable in a room or a bar, and she's always connecting people. Angel's been to the henna studios at the mall before. She says they are relaxed spaces where women hang out for hours—they are good places for conversation.

We go early to the mall on a Sunday morning. It's already crowded. There's a sign outside that says "A Somali Mall." The large group of men gathered outside laugh and talk over each other in Somali (I assume). Music is piped loudly inside and out—a woman's voice, not backed by instruments. I haven't been to Mogadishu, but I have been to African markets in Mali—and this feels like an African market more than Minnesota. The narrow halls are lined with stalls selling fabric in vibrant colors, jewelry, perfume, abayas, hijabs, shoes, electronics, books, and hair products. It smells like spices, grilled meats, and frankincense.

The place where Angel got tattoos in the past isn't open yet, so we wander. Get in the elevator. Get out at the third floor. We don't know what we're doing.

When we get off the elevator, an elegant man steps out of his bookstall and asks if he can

I worried a little that if I followed Hagar into her Islamic terrain, I might be disappointed by all the patriarchy I'd find there. One way to avoid it, I decided, was to gather the stories of women.

help us. When I tell him we're interested in henna tattoos, he says he knows a great artist and introduces us to Amina. She leads us through the front room of her stall where beautiful dresses and some products like shampoo and soap are displayed. The back room is full of boxes and broken furniture.

Amina clears away empty packaging and water bottles to make room for us on a black vinyl couch with a missing leg. She sits on a milk crate in front of us and gets started with me.

She draws quickly—intricate patterns in black and red from my fingertips to my elbows.

Amina shrugs off our compliments about her skill. Every girl knows how to do the henna designs in Somalia, she says—there is nothing else to do—no school, so the girls sew. And do henna. She came to Minnesota from a refugee camp in Kenya. Amina pulls aside her hijab and lifts up her shirt to show us bullet wounds on her chest and upper left arm.

I am thinking that the Hagar story might not be very relevant to her life, but I blunder through some clumsy explanation of what I'm working on and ask if she's familiar with Hagar. Amina says she's not religious. She doesn't know anything about Hagar. More women come in. Amina makes the rounds, painting hands, and arms, and feet, and calves. While one pattern is drying she begins work on another.

The next five Muslim women that I meet on the Internet and over the phone also don't know Hagar. When I ask Meymun, a translator for a women's clinic in St. Cloud, if she has Muslim women role models, she tells me about Hawo Tako, a Somali freedom fighter, who died in a demonstration she led against an Italian colonial. A monument in Mogadishu honors her bravery. She also tells me about Asil Osman Abade, an air force pilot and civil rights activist. She knows of Hagar, but she wants me to know about these women.

"Saying Islam meaningfully," writes Shahab Ahmed in his book *What Is Islam?*, "requires making ourselves sensitive to the 'capaciousness, complexity and, often outright contradiction' that inheres within the broadest possible range of practices, beliefs, representational forms, metaphors, and objects associated with Islam." My knowledge is narrow. I am learning not to assume anything about a woman's faith because she identifies as Muslim.

The literal and inclusive definition of *Muslim* is "one who submits to God." It's a much more inclusive term than *Christian* or *Jewish*, each of which is far more specific. The history of Islam, according to Ahmed, is full of many different manifestations of Islamic belief. It "comprehends the literalism of textual restrictivists who give absolute priority to the text of the Koran and the Hadith (the corpus of sayings attributed to Muhammad)" as well as the expansivist projects of Islamic philosophers and Sufi mystics. It includes the celebration of figural representation and the banning of it. Some Islamic poetry overflows with references to the virtues of wine.

People's faith can be important to them in an infinite variety of ways, and it can also be peripheral to their identity. Of course, there are many people who identify as Christian who don't know the story of Abraham—or are not very interested in it. For some erroneous reason, I thought it would be easy to find a Muslim woman who wanted to talk about Hagar. It's not. But I keep looking.

Muhammad's Wives

I meet Hend Al Mansour at the gallery where she recently installed her exhibition: *Mihrab-Hermitage*. She practiced medicine in Saudi Arabia before coming to Minnesota, where she began to explore sculpture. She knows Hagar and ran between the hills of Safa and Marwah in Mecca, following in Hagar's footsteps. The experience filled her with a feeling of compassion, imagining Hagar running with her child in her arms.

Hend's wearing black jeans and a turtleneck sweater. Her hair is loose and kinky, dark with streaks of gray.

Hend respects Hagar and her place as a matriarch, but the Islamic stories that are most important to her are the ones about the wives and daughters of Muhammad. She likes the fact that Khadija, his first wife, was fifteen years older than Muhammad and that he was her employee. She likes that Muhammad stayed with her and her only until she died.

Khadija was a wealthy woman. She ran her husband's business after he died. In the sixth century, so the stories go, she hired her distant cousin Muhammad ibn Abdullah to work for her. He was an excellent employee. Though many wealthy men had proposed to her after she was widowed, she wanted to marry Muhammad. *She* proposed. He accepted.

Around this time, according to the Islamic founding narratives, things were changing in Arabia. An influx of money and trade was interfering with the nomadic values of community. A new sort of individualism was on the rise. Troubled by the growing economic disparity and the erosion of community and concerned that people were neglecting to care for the vulnerable, Muhammad went to a cave outside of Mecca to fast and pray.

Sleeping in the cave one night, he was awakened by a divine presence commanding him to "recite." He was terrified. Like Moses or Jeremiah, Muhammad refused the command to speak, believing he was incapable of channeling the divine word. But the presence kept pressing him, so he began to speak the words that over time became the Qur'an, or the Recitation.

Overwhelmed by the experience, Muhammad made his way home, back to Khadija. He threw himself into her lap and asked her to protect him from this presence. She comforted him, confident that this presence meant to help him restore the generous and loving community his people had lost. Khadija convinced Muhammad that God was with him—that he should proceed and not be afraid. According to tradition, this is where the Islamic faith begins (610 CE).

Working and traveling for Khadija, Muhammad came in contact with Christian and Jewish communities. He had heard of the God of Abraham, and it was this God, he believed, who spoke to him.

Because Muhammad couldn't write, the people who listened to his words memorized them. It wasn't until twenty years after his death that the first official compilation of the revelations he received was made.

Muhammad remained married monogamously to Khadija for twenty-five years until her death. After Khadija died, Muhammad "went crazy" according to Hend, marrying many women—twelve, to be exact. But it wasn't like he was collecting trophy wives. Most were widows. Sawda bint Zam'a was said to be fifty-five when he married her. One wife was Christian, and one was Jewish. Muhammad was surrounded by women—old women, young women, Christian women, Jewish women. His closest offspring was his youngest daughter by Khadija, Fatimah. He had no sons that lived past infancy. As Amy Poppinga, a history teacher, said to me, "his whole life was women."

His youngest wife, Aisha, was "brilliant and feisty," according to Hend. She lived for forty-four years after Muhammad died and was instrumental in collecting the hadith, the sayings or narratives about Muhammad's words and deeds not included in the Qur'an but essential to informing

Islamic law. Aisha didn't write the hadith, but she relayed them, collected them, and verified which sayings were true. In many respects, Aisha is the most important person in the development of the hadith. A woman. If there is a woman behind any of the canonical writings in the Jewish or Christian traditions, we never hear of her. Aisha "had Muhammad's ear," according to Poppinga. She challenged him on things. She argued with men about what should be written. At one point she even pulled an army together to avenge the murder of the third caliph. She led the troops from the back of her camel.

Mihrab-Hermitage: Making Female Spaces

Mihrabs, the prayer niches found in mosques, orient worshippers toward Mecca. They are beautiful spaces covered in elaborate mosaics, but mihrabs are typically for men; Hend says it is more common for women to pray at home. The mihrabs she has installed in the gallery are for and about women. Hend doesn't practice the traditional Islamic prayer because she feels there are too many restrictions—for instance, a woman has to wear the veil to pray. Hend doesn't wear a veil. Her spaces don't read as restrictive—they are both reverent and playful, spacious enough to host a child's tea party but intimate enough to feel womblike. Her mihrabs represent the passions of the different Muslim women Hend interviewed—from Saudi Arabia, Syria, and Morocco. Each alcove has a hand-painted prayer rug and central image that reflects what each of the women identified as a crucial element of her identity—Sisterhood, Motherhood, and Freedom.

The visual art is accompanied by a recording of a woman's voice singing the traditional Islamic call to prayer. Hend says it still sounds strange to her ears because you never hear the call sung by a woman. It's always a man. I imagine how hearing this call five times a day would draw me away from my computer and my phone and remind me to be grateful.

Hend tells me about the goddesses worshiped at Mecca before the rise of Islam. The Banat al-lah, or the Daughters of the God, were very popular deities among the Arabs. According to Hend, Muhammad did not want to make war or have disagreements with the people who loved the Banat al-lah, so as they were negotiating, he said it would be all right if they still worshiped the goddesses. Muhammad says, "These are the exalted cranes whose intercession is to be hoped for," as if they are okay and it is okay to hope for their intercession. But later Gabriel comes to tell him that when he spoke these words, the devil was whispering in his ear. These are the so-called Satanic Verses.

Several biographers of Muhammad record this story, but the historicity of the incident is not accepted by most Muslims scholars today because they have determined the chain of narrators who relate the incident is unreliable. The story is also incompatible with the doctrine of prophetic infallibility—Muhammad makes a mistake. Hend likes the story. She sees it as a sign connecting Muhammad with the divine feminine.

Hend says the Ka'aba, the holy shrine at Mecca, is female—that's how it's referred to, as a she. Hend describes the ceremony where the Ka'aba's dressing is changed. A black silk and gold curtain covers the Ka'aba, called the *Kiswa*. When the Kiswa is replaced, the new dress is pulled down before the old one is taken away. Hend says they treat the Ka'aba as if it is a modest woman—a self-conscious older woman, or a shy young bride who doesn't want her bare skin to show as she changes her clothes.

Arabs had been making pilgrimages to Mecca, circling the sacred Ka'aba, long before Muhammad's day—so long, that the original meaning of the rites had been all but lost. Instead of forbidding these ancient practices, Muhammad reinterpreted them so that people would recognize that the one God, the God of the Christians and Jews—the God for all people, had always been behind them. According to Muhammad's vision, the sacred place was where Abraham started his Arabic family.

Hend says she doesn't always like the surface of Islam, but she loves what is underneath. She believes in what is underneath the surface.

The traditions surrounding the Ka'aba remind me of the stories that surround Christian relics or holy sites, or Christmas or Easter for that matter. There are so many layers. We know the church placed its most important feasts on days that coincided with traditional religious practices: Epiphany on the day of the Isis festival, Christmas near the winter solstice—when people celebrated the birth of the sun god, Easter at the time of ancient spring festivities. Instead of worrying about how the monotheistic meaning supplants all the lingering vestiges of Indigenous meaning, we might celebrate how the layering ties us to our ancient ancestors and the rhythms of the planet—the migration of birds, the flowering of trees, the amount of light in our days. It reminds us that we are earthly creatures and that God's love is present in every layer—the rambunctious deity behind or underneath all. We're always going to be a little off, but that doesn't mean God isn't there—behind, underneath, getting through to us.

Hend promises to let me know how her work progresses—when there will be new mihrabs on display. I want to bow to her instead of shaking her hand when she holds it out to me—to honor her for taking paint, and paper, and fabric, using glue and scissors, to create these spaces for mothers, and sisters, and immigrant daughters—for giving physical expression to this tangible need.

5 Full Faith and Effort

Where I Meet a Feminist Muslim Scholar

> Islam is, at its core, a religion of dissent. It is not premised on an endless list of do's and don't's, but is instead multifarious and openly accepting of multiplicity.
>
> —Asma T. Uddin

> Islam is the first feminism.
>
> —Anse Tamara Gray

The woman in charge of Islamic relationships at the Minnesota Council of Churches gets me in touch with Anse Tamara Gray. Gray is the founder of Rabata, an Islamic organization "dedicated to promoting positive cultural change through individual empowerment, spiritual upbringing of women by women, and the revival of the female voice in scholarship." I'm not sure what to expect when I meet with her at Daylight, the bookstore she runs.

When Anse Tamara (Anse is a traditional Syrian word for teacher) arrives for our meeting, she's wearing a hijab and jilbab, a long navy blue garment that looks like a raincoat. If I could see her hair, I'm guessing from her coloring it might be red. The shop is playing the music of Mumford and Sons. It's full of children's books, scholarly books, books of poetry, and novels—there is a place to make tea and soft couches to sit on.

Anse Tamara grew up Lutheran in the suburbs of the Twin Cities. I ask if she minds talking about how she became a Muslim. She says, "Not at all. It was a feminist crisis." She became an advocate for female empowerment as soon as she was conscious of inequality. Her faith was also important to her, but the summer before she began college, she realized that she couldn't be a Christian any longer because she couldn't worship a man. My heart leapt a little—to hear someone put it like that—so matter of fact. For her the crisis wasn't angry or righteous—she didn't want to give up her faith, but when she studied the early Christian councils that established the creeds that form the basis for Christian practice and belief, it disturbed her that all the contours of Christian faith were decided by "a bunch of men sitting around a table."

It wasn't that she was willfully discarding her upbringing; she was having a crisis of faith. She didn't want to live in the world without faith, so she thought, "The only way out of this is to learn." She began to look at every religion other than Islam, because she knew Islam was oppressive to women, so she wasn't going to bother. But then she came across some verses in the Qur'an that she found incredibly egalitarian. In the Qur'an both sexes are created deliberately and independently. There is no mention of Eve being created out of Adam's rib. And Adam is as much the first sinner as Eve. The Qur'an clearly establishes the equality of men and women. Surah 3:195 says, "I shall not lose sight of the labor of any of you who labors in My way, be it man or woman; each of you is equal to the other."

Hyper-smart, extroverted, articulate, she laughs loudly and has a very large presence that might be intimidating, except that she is also disarmingly warm. Tamara says she discovered that patriarchy was not essential to Islam. In fact, she says, "Islam is the first feminism." She said that Islam in its earliest manifestations is a community of equality. The first years were revolutionary for women.

> *In the Qur'an both sexes are created deliberately and independently. There is no mention of Eve being created out of Adam's rib. And Adam is as much the first sinner as Eve. The Qur'an clearly establishes the equality of men and women.*

The Qur'an, composed in the seventh century, affirms rights for women that were rarely recognized elsewhere until the nineteenth century. Before Islam, women were treated like property in the Arab world. Islam came and changed all that. The Qur'an stipulates that women can own property, form contracts, divorce, and have a say in who they marry. Muhammad insisted that education was an obligation for men and women. Tamara says that in regions where Islamic women are oppressed, such treatment is a result of cultural norms that have persisted in spite of, rather than because of, true Islamic teaching.

After studying the Qur'an and recognizing its egalitarian qualities, Anse Tamara said she was "desperate to learn." But she didn't immediately find an environment friendly to women. She thought, "These people needed to learn their religion."

While many of the Muslim women I spoke to said that Muhammad's wives were inspirational female figures in their faith, Anse Tamara said she is not that impressed with the stories about them. She loves that they are known as the Mothers of Believers. She loves the part they play in Muhammad's life, but what is written about them is often flat, she thinks—too focused on how they were good wives. For her they are not merely good wives—they are the first female scholars.

She's excited to talk about Hagar. I'm excited that she's excited. She leans forward with her elbows on her knees, her hands clasped in front of her. She looks at me intensely like she is about to deliver a message of profound gravity. She says, "We have in this tradition this woman—if any man, woman, or child, especially man—but anyone—if they want to complete the five pillars of Islam, they have to imitate a woman." Hagar's activity is the crux of hajj, or pilgrimage. There is no hajj without Hagar—without her running from one mountain to another.

In Islamic tradition, Hagar's expulsion from Abraham's household isn't an episode of female oppression; it is a part of God's plan to establish a sanctuary in the desert along with rituals that pilgrims will follow as long as the world endures. Nor is Hagar a victim. She had to face distress and danger, as do most of God's historical agents. Like God's prophets, she persists, and so her name and memory came to be a part of Islam's sacred history and rituals. She is Hager the believer, the Mother, the Matriarch who stands at the beginning of the Islamic story.

Hagar's running may be seen as her test, Tamara says, a trial analogous to the one met by Abraham when he was asked to sacrifice his son. "Hagar is left in Mecca, alone with her baby." In Islamic tradition, Tamara says, "Ishmael is one and a half years old. Hagar is left to fend for herself and her son.

But she has the intellectual capacity to do this. In the desert. Alone with no one."

Tamara chooses her words to describe Hagar deliberately. She says Hagar's action is "an expression of full trust and effort." I have imagined Hagar running between the hills in a panic, but Tamara says it is a very calculated effort. It is not frantic. She is looking for a caravan. She knows this is the only way she and her son will survive.

Tamara says Hagar is "a lioness for her child," adding, "The mother-and-child bond is very internal. Very deep. A woman might give up looking for the caravan in the desert if it was just for herself, but wanting to save her child's life, she will not give up."

Hagar, according to Tamara, "doesn't get angry with God. She is also not passive. She doesn't passively wait for someone else to do something—realizes the only way she will survive is to find a caravan. She participates in the 'saving' process—running back and forth from one high spot to the next." Tamara says this is the metaphor in this sacred story—this balance between effort and trust. "She has her son to protect. She is exhausted from the effort but there is no narration that she sat down in despair. As if she had given up. She sits down in wonder," says Tamara, "wonder and curiosity. What's going to happen?"

I can't imagine I would feel "wonder and curiosity" if I were left alone in the desert with my dying child, but I love the image of a woman with a trust so profound that she recognizes she doesn't need to be afraid—ultimately, somehow, it will be okay. Fear not, for I am with you. Yea, though I walk through the valley of the shadow of death—that sort of thing. A balance of trust and effort might be just the thing to pull us through these difficult days.

Imagine the Trust

"Every Muslim everywhere," Tamara says, "makes note of what Hagar has done. It is a woman who sets the example of full trust and effort." If you die never having followed in Hagar's footsteps, your kids can do it for you. If you are too poor, someone can make the hajj on your behalf. If you are not at the hajj because you have already gone, you still celebrate what the pilgrims there are doing. So every single year you're talking about Hagar, thinking about what she did. You are remembering her story.

"Pilgrims must imitate Hagar fully. Fully. From a feminist lens," she says, "This is amazing. If you make a mistake in hajj, and don't follow Hagar well, if you don't do it the way she did it, you have to pay. The money goes to help the poor. It's a matter of starting in the right place and ending in the right place. Going at the speed she went.

"The way Saudis have made it now, to accommodate so many pilgrims, it is not like you really climb the mountains Hagar climbed, but you must go up. Going up to the top is best, but at least you must climb some stairs," she says. Pilgrims walk at a normal pace until they reach two green pillars, which mark a short section of the path where they run.

When I imagined the hajj, I pictured desert hills and rocky paths. Tamara tells me it's not much like that these days. The

If you die never having followed in Hagar's footsteps, your kids can do it for you. If you are too poor, someone can make the hajj on your behalf. If you are not at the hajj because you have already gone, you still celebrate. So every single year you're remembering her story.

whole route is paved in white marble now and entirely en-
closed in air-conditioned tunnels as part of the Grand Mosque
complex. I imagined the Zamzam well as a stream people
would bend down to drink from, but actually the water from
the well is piped in from a purification plant, bottled, and
made available in coolers throughout the mosque.

Hagar is not named specifically in the Qur'an, but she is
present as the mother of Ishmael. Later commentators flesh
out her story, filling in detail. In addition to the Qur'an, Muslims have Tafsir (interpretations of qur'anic verses similar to
Jewish midrash) and the hadith (the collection of originally
oral stories that contain sayings of Muhammad and accounts
of his activities). There are also respected histories.

Wafa, a dentist I met through the Muslim Society of
America, relates one of the Hagar stories to me. When Abraham leaves Hagar in the desert she asks, "Are you leaving us
here?" He doesn't answer. She asks again, "So you're really
leaving us here?" He doesn't answer. Finally, as he is leaving,
Hagar calls out to him one last time, "O Abraham, I ask you
three times who commanded you to set me down in a land
without grain, without cows' udders, without people, without water, and without provisions?" He said, "My Lord commanded me." Once she knows it is God behind it, according
to Wafa, she accepts it.

She's a little bit incredulous, a little bit demanding—like,
"Abraham, you've got to be kidding me: No cows' udders or
water or other people?" She might not entirely trust Abraham,
but she trusts God, Wafa says.

Practice Being Graceful

Tamara says she has experienced Muslim environments that are not egalitarian, but she doesn't want to disempower men with her feminism. Black men and Muslim men (and Black Muslim men!) have been disempowered enough, she says. Eighty percent of Muslim countries were colonized. She described watching what a man has to go through in Syria, for example, just to pay his power bill—bribes, corruption, negotiations. She says it won't do any good to disempower men.

She had difficulty finding her place in the mosques in Minnesota when she first converted. Eventually she met a woman who came from a long line of Syrian women scholars. In the course of time, Tamara married the woman's brother and moved to Damascus, Syria, for twenty years, where she received classic training as an Islamic scholar, studying Islamic sacred texts and subjects including: Shāfiʿī jurisprudence, Islamic theology, qurʾanic sciences, Arabic grammar, geography of the Muslim world, Islamic civilization and culture, Islamic history, and classical methods of spiritual growth.

Bringing out what is joyful in Islam is important to her. As is making significant cultural change. Whereas practicing Muslims might not listen to academic feminists trained in the West, they are more likely to be open to her classic training. She runs an online seminary that enrolls four hundred women. She has hosted storytelling workshops and Native-Muslim prayer meetings to support the Water Protectors at Standing Rock. She teaches academic courses and leads spiritual retreats.

Anse Tamara is careful not to speak disparagingly about anything or anyone—not her Lutheran upbringing, not Islamic men, not even Donald Trump, not the detrimental effects of colonization. For her it is more matter of fact. The scientific, literary, mathematical, architectural, philosophical, and medical achievements throughout Islamic history were vast and innovative. Some say the Islamic world, during its Golden Age, was the first truly universal civilization, gathering scholars and artists from every ethnic origin and religion together to advance many disciplines. Nevertheless, European colonialists, beginning with Napoleon's invasion of Egypt in 1798, saw Muslim society as inferior and corrupt and expressed their contempt in myriad ways. Nearly every Muslim country was conquered and colonized by foreign powers.

Americans are often bewildered by the hostility expressed by some Muslims for Western culture, but the contempt that Westerners have displayed for Islamic culture thickly inhabits history.

Tamara and I talk past the hour we have scheduled. I thank her for her time. She recommends some books and says I should stay and browse. I page through a thin volume with beautiful photos and few words. It's a sort of introduction to Islam for people who are not acquainted with it. I pause at the pictures of a broad range of women from many cultures with different head coverings.

The text points out that these are all Islamic head coverings. A Nigerian woman wears a colorful kerchief in bold African print tied around her head. It matches her dress. A young girl from Kazakhstan models a very cute hat, like one missionaries brought back to my parents when I was a child. I never thought of it as an Islamic head covering. I'm sure my parents didn't either—they let me wear it to church and school. Another image shows a woman from Bulgaria with a scarf tied under her chin—an Eastern European look.

Looking at these pictures after talking with a devout Muslim feminist made me realize how little I know about so many things and how important it is to remember that.

The text between the photographs says, "Public displays of the body may enrich the fashion and cosmetic industries, but they are oppressively marginalizing to the old—and to all who physically fail to measure up to the current images of perfection. In this way, modesty is seen as liberating rather than oppressive." For a moment, I wish for a hijab for my next birthday. I haven't found that there's a ton of respect out there for the aging female body. Attitudes are oppressive. I hear people talk about events or churches where there are "just a bunch of old ladies." (Like we all know what that means.) I've done it myself. In my culture, mature women are not generally considered powerfully important human beings (although there are exceptions, if you are Helen Mirren or Ruth Bader Ginsberg). But looking at the pictures of all these Muslim women, many from cultures that honor elders, I was moved to recognize the varieties of liberation that practicing faith can mean.

6 Iftar
Visiting a Mosque with my Daughter

Next time someone sees her in *hijab*, she concludes, "Don't look at me sympathetically. I am not under duress or a male-worshipping female captive from those barbarous Arabic deserts. I've been liberated."

—Sultana Yusufali

Generous listening is powered by curiosity, a virtue we can invite and nurture in ourselves to render it instinctive. It involves a kind of vulnerability—a willingness to be surprised, to let go of assumptions and take in ambiguity.

—Krista Tippett

Taking Heart is a program in the Twin Cities started in 2005 to bring Christians and Muslims together to get to know each other over a meal. Muslims invite non-Muslims into their mosques and community spaces to share in the evening meal that breaks the Ramadan fast, an Iftar dinner. Olivia and I plan to go to one together, but as is often the case with a seventeen-year-old daughter, when it's actually time to go, it feels like I have foisted this on her. She puts on her headphones for the hour and a half drive.

We park by the mosque—housed in a nondescript, corporate looking building in an industrial office park. I was illogically hoping for a minaret.

After we're graciously greeted by an older woman and kind man—after we feel the plush and pretty carpet under our feet—after five or more people eagerly, hospitably race to find us a chair, I'm gratified that Olivia leans over and whispers in my ear that she is so happy to be here. (Afterwards she tells me that the call to prayer was so beautiful that tears came to her eyes, "and the way the people said Allah was such a revelation—so musical.")

After prayer a young man gives a presentation for the visitors about Ramadan. He reminds me of almost every evangelical youth group leader I've ever met—enthusiastic and sincere, wrapped in a not very convincing cloak of cool. More charisma than gravity.

He makes a very tame joke about sex. He's talking about what you fast from during Ramadan—food, drink, and intercourse—from sunup to sundown. He says these are all needs, but obviously abstaining from these things is harder for some people than others, and then he wiggles and raises his eyebrows. It's really not a very funny joke, but everyone laughs. It feels like church.

I like it when he talks about the practice of praying five times a day. He calls it meditation. It reminds him God is present wherever he is—reminds him to be grateful. He says a lot of the practice of Islam—always saying "God willing" or "Inshallah," always thanking God—these are ways to keep aware of the continuous connection between oneself and God. He says Ramadan is about cultivating gratitude, attention, and generosity.

Next he talks about God's mercy. He says in Islam there are ninety-nine names for God, emphasizing God's most important characteristics, and the most important is "God, the Merciful." God's mercy is emphasized over all other aspects of God.

He says that during Ramadan, Satan is absent—the devils are shackled. I'm not sure what he means, but I like imagining there could be a time of year when people are not influenced by greed or selfishness. It doesn't seem like a bad practice—this imagining—like we all might get busy while the devils are shackled, while we have this moment free.

When it's time to eat, Olivia leads the line. Normally, she might hang back in an unfamiliar situation, but she's hungry from fasting, which makes her brash and dauntless. It's a side of her I like to see. One of the young women serving rice and chicken has on jeans, a hijab, and a T-shirt that says Legit Hijabi. Olivia tells her she likes her shirt. She stretches it out to let us have a better look and says she likes Olivia's nails, which are painted bright red.

There are a lot of visitors this day—mostly women. Olivia and I sit down at a table with three older women, who are friends through their church, Zamzam from the mosque, who is about Olivia's age, and Nancy, a retired elementary school teacher with dyed red hair and her lipstick on crooked. No one has an agenda. The conversation is easy. Nancy jokes with Zamzam that at least she doesn't have to worry about bad hair days. Zamzam laughs. She's wearing a scarf made from emerald green fabric with luminescent golden flowers. She says, "Well, actually I have a hat that says 'Bad Hijab Day.'" Sometimes it's hard to get the hijab pinned down right, so she throws on the hat over it.

All the women at our table have memories of when women in their churches wore hats or little kerchiefs to cover their heads. Nancy says she went to a wedding at a Catholic church just three years ago where the women covered their heads.

Many young Muslim women choose to wear hijab as a rebellion against consumer capitalism, with its objectification and commodification of the female body, according to Katherine Bullock in her book *Rethinking Muslim Women and the Veil*. They see hijab "as an empowering tool of resistance."

I ask Zamzam about her name and she tells me about Hagar's well. She tells me that you can buy Zamzam water in Muslim stores right here in Minnesota. If you pray while you drink it, some people say, your prayers will be answered. It is supposed to satisfy thirst and hunger. She said she drank it once and then she wasn't hungry, but she's not sure. She's not completely convinced that this is true, that the water has these benefits, but she is also not convinced it is false.

Zamzam and Olivia talk about school and homework. Zamzam wants to study something in college that will enable her to do some good in the world—help her community, but also help her to support her family.

Olivia remarks that the women really seem to be in charge at the mosque. She says she liked it that the young man who spoke kept deferring to one of the older women when he couldn't answer a question. Zamzam tells us there is no real hierarchy in the mosque. Various people lead the prayer. There is an imam, but she says she didn't even know who he was for certain until recently.

When we're finished eating, we take pictures together. Zamzam and Olivia decide to follow each other on Instagram. I never had a sense during this conversation among women that our difference in belief was a pressing problem—we were curious about each other and had little interest in debate. My father admits to being Islamophobic, but I wonder whether, if he had the opportunity to worship with Muslims, eat with Muslims, or have a conversation with a Muslim, he would find his fear fading.

Finding Spaces

We find our place in Scripture even if it involves wrestling something out from under the surface. Maybe sometimes all it takes is a flashlight—sometimes a crow bar, maybe a jackhammer. Sometimes it is a quiet shift—sometimes it is disruptive. Just as Hagar established a community in a barren land, we make spaces for ourselves out of plastic and paint—our own prayer niches, a women's seminary, and a bookstore.

Hagar's legacy is not a neat package—it's sprawling. But I am grateful to have the image of the mother running up and down hills to find water for her thirsty child. I can relate to it better than the image of the father being willing to kill his son for his god.

Hagar's legacy is not a neat package—it's sprawling. But I am grateful to have this matriarch to think about when I think about faith: the image of the mother running up and down hills to find water for her thirsty child. I can relate to it better than the image of the father being willing to kill his son for his god.

Maybe it's because Muslims have such a prominent matriarch as Hagar that the place of the mother in Islam often surpasses that of the father. "Paradise lies at the feet of the mother," Muhammad says. There's a story in the hadith where Muhammad is asked, "Who should be my most honored companion?" Muhammad says, "Your mother." "Who next?" the inquirer asks. Muhammad says, "Your mother." Okay then, asks the disciple, "Who after that?" Muhammad says, "Your mother." Only on the fourth time does Muhammad mention the father.

I know nothing is ever uncomplicated, but focusing on the mother can shift the way we read our sacred stories—make a way when it seems like there is no way.

Part Three

Esther

7 The Biblical Story
The Jewish Heroine Who Reclaims Eros

> For I conclude that the enemy is not lipstick, but guilt it-
> self; we deserve lipstick, if we want it, AND free speech;
> we deserve to be sexual AND serious—or whatever we
> please. We are entitled to wear cowboy boots to our own
> revolution.
>
> —Naomi Wolf

It doesn't happen all that often, but when it does you'd think I
might be prepared. Someone asks me who my role models are.
I blank, panic a little, and then name some women writers or
theologians I love. The truth is, I don't have role models, exactly.

People are amazing, and crazy, and admirable, and capable
of beautiful and terrible things—all of us, everyone. I learn
more than I could ever say from writers and biblical scholars,
and my friends and teachers, and my parents and children,
and my cats and dogs, and even wild animals. But role models? It's a lot of responsibility to impose on a person. We all
shine and we all fail. We are often not on our best behavior.
Most of us don't hold up well under scrutiny. It's part of what
it means to be humans in need of the grace of God.

"Role model" wouldn't have been an expression that the
biblical authors were kicking around. The term was coined

in the 1970s by sociologist Robert K. Merton. The idea was that, in order to succeed in careers, women and minorities needed role models—examples of people like them who had succeeded. The role-model idea may make sense as a twentieth-century concept for people looking to achieve workplace equity, but it isn't a great frame to bring to biblical literature.

Characters in the Bible may reveal a truth about the human condition or what it's like to be a human in relationship with God. They are inspirational at times. But as for figures we're meant to emulate? David slept with another man's wife and proceeded to have the man killed. Ezekiel ate a scroll and lay on his left side for 390 days. Hosea named his children "Unloved" and "Not My People." The disciples betrayed Jesus at his most crucial hour. The characters in the Bible are wonderfully and terribly human.

The law helps us know how to live in relationship to God and each other. The prophets exhort us to come back to relationship when we fail. The characters of the Bible show us how surprisingly complicated the path can sometimes be.

People have been passing judgment on Esther for a long time. She doesn't resist being taken into a harem quite enough. She hides her Jewish identity. Either she's too sexy or she isn't a good feminist. She may not hold up perfectly well under scrutiny, but we need a matriarch like her: a matriarch who is not a mother—who saves, not her children but her people. A matriarch who may not be a natural-born leader, but who acts in a crucial moment, beyond even her own expectations for herself, through unsanctioned means to keep her people from destruction. And she does this in a world where God is hidden—apparently silent. She is not a likely hero, perhaps, but in the midst of violent oppression set in place by foolish men, she acts with bravery. We need her.

Barbie Doll or Prophetess

The number of times men wanted to cut Esther out of Scripture makes me like her all the more. The book of Esther is the only one from the Hebrew Bible not found among the Dead Sea Scrolls. Some people conjecture this is because the community at Qumran would have looked down on her for marrying a Persian. (And it could be because they were humorless ascetics.) For eight hundred years Christianity was virtually silent on the book. John Calvin didn't include it in his biblical commentaries. Martin Luther said, "I am so great an enemy to . . . Esther, that I wish it had not come to us at all." He felt it had too much "Judaizing" and too much "pagan naughtiness."

The rabbis, on the other hand, couldn't stop talking about her. They comment on the book of Esther more than any other book in the Bible besides Genesis. Some of the comments were arguments over whether it should be included in Scripture. Some rabbis believed it had less sanctity than other books, while other rabbis rebuked them for this. At one point in the Talmud, Esther steps out of the pages of Scripture and argues for herself, demanding that the rabbis "commemorate me for future generations." They resist, but she insists—effectively challenging the authority of the rabbis and winning. This is one of the beautiful sorts of things that happen in midrash. The rabbinic interpreters are not afraid to question their own authority or to not always agree. Their way of truth-seeking is very different from the way Western

Christian tradition has conceived of it. Truth isn't so much static or singular—it's something one finds in argument or conversation—by asking questions.

In seminary I learned that the goal of interpretation was not to question the text as much as uncover the original author's intended meaning. One could ask about genre or historical context, but not so much about the gaps in the narrative. There was a limit to the sorts of questions that were appropriate to a text. We weren't encouraged to read a text creatively. From the rabbis, I learned to approach a text with unfettered curiosity. Imagine Esther stepping out of the book and fighting with the rabbis!

Ultimately, Esther secures her place in the canon and more—she is listed in the Talmud as the last of the seven prophetesses even though she never actually receives a direct message from God.

Maimonides, a medieval Sephardic Jewish philosopher and foremost commentator on the Torah, says that in the age to come, when the light of the Messiah shines unobstructed, when the books of the prophets and the other sacred writings have been suspended—when they cease to be read in public, the scroll of Esther will continue to have vitality. Ancient troubles will be remembered no more, but the days of Purim, the festival of Esther, will be celebrated into infinity.

A mere thirteen verses from the book of Esther appear in the Revised Common Lectionary. And these are read only once in a three-year cycle. Jewish communities, on the other hand, read the book in its entirety every year at the festival of Purim.

Lately, Christians have been warming toward Esther, if the number of books from Christian publishers is any measure of that. Such books include Bible studies for women and teen girls, self-help books, and romance novels based on the story of Esther. In the 2008 presidential campaign, vice presidential nominee Sarah Palin claimed Esther as a role model—like Esther, she saw herself as part of a persecuted religious minority whose time had come to save her nation from corruption. Evangelical appropriation of Esther has become a thing.

Maimonides says that in the age to come, the scroll of Esther will continue to have vitality. Ancient troubles will be remembered no more, but the days of Purim, the festival of Esther, will be celebrated into infinity.

This swell of interest may be part of the reason a woman rabbi I contact doesn't really want to talk to me. I ask her if she's named after Esther. She says no, she's named after her grandmother. She says she is not interested in Esther nor does she think she's an important character. For her, Esther is like a Jewish Barbie doll or Jewish Disney princess. She says that she isn't a biblical scholar and she doesn't know a lot about Esther and that other people might feel differently, but for her Purim is an unimportant holiday for children.

Rabbi Alan Shavit-Lonstein, on the other hand, thinks Esther is a great heroine for little girls. Shavit-Lonstein is the founder of an interfaith organization in St. Paul and a certified Genius at the Apple Store. He met me for lunch after a long morning of helping people with their iPhones. He says little girls start to love Esther when they are in their princess phase. "She has all that element: beauty, crown, lives in a palace, attended by eunuchs—but she is also an incredibly positive political actor." She is a powerful example of someone who risks her life to act in the face of injustice. The Elizabeth Warren meme was going around at the time. Rabbi Alan said, "Esther is like Elizabeth Warren: she violated the rules. She was warned. Nevertheless she persisted."

More Beyoncé than Betty Friedan

I've been thinking of Esther as the vamp of the resistance, a truly alternative tale for the likes of the canon. Hagar is the determined matriarch. Esther's role in the revolution is different. Her name is a derivative of Ishtar, who is, after all, a goddess of love. After reading her story, a young writer from my church said, "She must have been the world's greatest lover." She saves her people from the threat of annihilation because, the text suggests, she sexually pleases the king so immensely. I'm not sure I'd want all the young girls in our church setting out to follow in her footsteps, but what an interesting reversal from your average saint. She embraces the erotic.

We need her in our triumvirate—for all the lipstick-loving, high-heel-wearing, anti-sex-shaming, sex-positive advocates—for those seeking relief from patriarchal strictures on women's sexuality—for every woman ever called a slut. It's surprising and refreshing to meet such a woman in the pages of our holy book.

The Reverse Occurred

I'm happy when Rabbi Adam Stock Spilker from Mt. Zion Temple in St. Paul welcomes me to attend a book study he is leading for his congregation on Esther. After the study there will be a Purim spiel, a comic dramatization of the Esther story. Mt. Zion is calling theirs *Esther: A Persian Musical.* It's a parody of the smash Broadway musical, *Hamilton.* I am definitely interested. Though my encounter with Jewish interpretive methods has been life-changing, I've never actually been to a Jewish community's Bible study.

We need Esther in our triumvirate—for all the lipstick-loving, high-heel-wearing, anti-sex-shaming, sex-positive advocates—for those seeking relief from patriarchal strictures on women's sexuality— for every woman ever called a slut.

When I walk into the classroom, more of a boardroom with an enormous table in the middle, I meet a lively bunch of people that crosses generations. The rabbi is wearing blue breeches, white stockings, pointed shoes, a waistcoat, cravat, and wig—like Thomas Jefferson or some other colonial gentleman. Someone wheels in a cart loaded with bottles of Sam Adams beer to go with the *Hamilton* theme. The rabbi hands out pages of notes for us entitled, "A Festive and Yet Quite Serious Study," which sums it up pretty well—though festive is the reigning mood.

A cheerful older man, wearing Birkenstocks and a bow-tie, comes to sit beside me. He introduces himself and asks if he can grab me a beer. After he hands me the drink, he sort of throws up his hands like, "Isn't it all so crazy?" "Maybe," he says, "we can smoke, too." The woman next to me says she came to Purim as Queen Esther for years, decked out in a fancy dress and loads of jewelry. This year her costume is minimal—a hat piled with flowers and rimmed with little multi-colored blinking lights like people wear at concerts and raves (I think). (I've never been to a rave.) I like this context for studying the Bible.

The rabbi begins, "Esther is not a simple book. The more time you spend with it, the more complex it gets—depth, meanings, layers—every time you think you understand it? There's a little more to it." But at the end of the day, he says, it is a comedy—a farce meant to provoke the audience to laughter. He thinks Esther 9:1 sums up the entire book, "The reverse occurred."

On the day the Jews expected their enemies to subdue them, the opposite happened—their sorrow was turned into laughter. The book institutes the holiday of Purim, which is both a celebration of survival, he says, and a day to break rules. Rabbi Spilker says it has a lot in common with Mardi Gras and other antinomian holidays when the ruling order is challenged—the status quo overthrown. He said, "We are such a law-abiding people, but we can't keep it up all the time. All year the Jews obey the law, and then on Purim, we let loose a little."

Thus the beer, the costumes, and the smoking (that actually never happens). When Sarah Palin identified herself as a type of Esther, I don't believe she was thinking of raucous subversion.

Scripture Can Be Funny

I never heard, growing up Baptist, that the book of Esther was funny—though it's hard to miss when I read the story now. I wonder if that's in part why Esther was ignored for so long in Christianity—like we couldn't deal with the idea that Scripture could be funny.

One of Nietzsche's most penetrating critiques of Christianity was that Christians were a joyless people. Paul Tillich said he almost left the faith for the same reason. The Bible is a compilation of stories, poetry, and questionable history about an enigmatic but graceful God who seeks relationship with humans: self-important creatures who fluctuate perpetually between grandiosity and shame—mammals who spend an inordinate amount of time and resources trying to convince themselves and others they are something they are not (radiant, godlike, flawless, immortal, or innocent). Surely the whole premise of the Bible lends itself to humor on occasion. Christian commentary doesn't often see it this way.

The book of Esther may be the most glaring example of comedy in the Bible, but it's not the only place that's funny. Balaam meets a talking donkey. Jonah throws a temper tantrum under his little shrub. Tobit is blinded by a bird pooping in his eye. Jesus uses hyperbole, sarcasm, and irony. He's a mensch with chutzpah. I sometimes wonder if he was joking when he called Peter the rock on which the church is built. The rock sinks when it believes it can walk on water, and it crumbles in betrayal at a crucial moment. There's tragedy in it, of course, but maybe some comedy, too.

Rabbinic readings are more playful than what you find in, say, the New Interpreters Bible in the Christian tradition. Avivah Zornberg says, "The midrash invites us to read the text with the truest—that is with the least conventional, platitudinous, or even pious—understandings available to us." It creates space for honest, inquisitive, imaginative readings rather than imposing a numbing sense of prohibition. The story of Esther is funny, but if you are reading it piously, you might miss it. Maybe Calvin and Luther didn't like it so much because it makes fun of men. In an e-mail exchange I had with Rabbi Rob Cabelli, a chaplain at Grinnell College, he wrote, "The comedic aspect of the Esther story . . . truly underscores, through the theatre of the absurd, through *comedie noir*, just how foolish the men are, in their egotism, excruciating insecurity and pompous obliviousness." There's a place for that in a "holy" book. Perhaps the compilers of the canon knew that, by the time we got through Joshua and Judges, Samuel and Kings, Ezra and Nehemiah, we were going to need a laugh at the pretensions of self-important men.

After those self-important men comes a book about a woman—who without the help of father or brother or husband—without being pure or holy or virginal, stands in the eye of an ego-driven, farcical, man-made, nearly catastrophic storm, and acts to save her people from destruction.

Not Your Typical Saint

Esther doesn't conduct herself like someone who is zealous for the law of her people, but she becomes a Jewish heroine. She doesn't rise up from unsavory circumstances ringed with white blossoms of purity like the Catholic Saint Agnes, who was thrown into a brothel but remained, miraculously, immaculate. Esther is decidedly not a hero of the nunnish type. She is not the sort of woman Christian tradition has held up as an example of feminine virtue. She distinguishes herself as the most desirable member of a harem. Her beauty and sexuality are essential to her character in this story—she is not rising up at night and making meals for her household or caring for children.

Esther is a folktale more than history—a timeless farce full of men behaving badly. The king of the Persian Empire, the greatest king the world had ever known, according to the book of Esther, is an ineffectual, pompous buffoon, surrounded by a cadre of advisors who pander to his ego.

In the first chapters of the book, he is throwing a preposterously lavish six-month party so everyone will know how rich he is—to show off "the riches of his royal glory and the splendor and pomp of his majesty." He had special couches made of gold and silver for his guests to sit on and golden goblets for them to drink from. The wine poured freely. Perhaps there were other drugs involved. (It's unclear how anyone sustains six months of drunken revelry.)

To top off the extravagant debauchery, the drunken king summons his queen, Vashti, to parade in front of his guests wearing nothing but her crown. She refuses to concede. Though we hardly get a chance to know her, Queen Vashti's defiance gives her a special place in the hearts of many readers. Her refusal enrages, humiliates, and unhinges the king and strikes fear in the hearts of all the men in the palace. They fear that if women see that Vashti gets away with her dissent, the patriarchy might topple—it will cause all women to look with contempt upon their husbands. So they banish Vashti and immediately send out a decree demanding that all women, high and low, must treat their husbands with respect.

When we invited our wise bishop, Patricia Lull, to preach on Esther at House of Mercy, it was clear the comedic aspect of the book hadn't escaped her. When she read the verses about the edict to enforce women's good behavior, the congregation erupted in laughter—the issuing of such an edict, obviously, was preposterous.

Mark Driscoll, former pastor of Mars Hill Church in Seattle, believes Esther is a historical book. He describes the king in a sermon series on the book of Esther. He says, "Everybody who's rich, powerful, cool, he's it, add a zero. That's Xerxes . . . he's a big deal. He's a handsome guy. So whatever your picture, ladies, is of a really good-looking guy—that was Xerxes." He says that Xerxes was a dirty rich man, but believes that any man given the power would be the same way. "When no women are present and no rules in place, men become animals. Amen?"

I prefer the Veggie Tales version of the king as more in line with the spirit of the book of Esther. He's a doltish zucchini who speaks with the telltale voice of a slow thinker, sprays breath freshener in his mouth, and keeps looking at himself in the mirror—not exactly your powerfully handsome playboy. His little minion (an indeterminate vegetable) is obviously the one deciding things. In the Veggie Tales version, Vashti is banished for refusing to make the king a sandwich at three o'clock in the morning.

The Rise of Women against Supremacy

Rabbi Spilker, at the Mt. Zion book study, points out that the book has parallels to the Joseph story found in Genesis. Both are about characters who live outside of Israel. God does not speak directly in either story. The characters are both said to be exceptionally beautiful and both act to save their people. Klara Butting, a German biblical scholar, reflecting on these parallels, suggests that it would be "quite in order to assume that women took part in composing this retelling of Joseph's story"— women who recognized the need for old stories to be retold if they were going to continue to have meaning for evolving generations.

Thus imagined, she writes, the book of Esther reveals a "protest against the breaking and silencing of female power." It shows that "the rise of women against supremacy and oppression is essential" in order to keep generation after generation from falling into the same patterns of violence against women—violence against the Jewish people. The story links the fight against sexist power and the fight for liberation of Jewish people from anti-Semitic threat, according to Butting. The rise of women against supremacy is essential—of course it is.

One of the Most Beautiful Women Ever Created

After the king's anger against Vashti settles down, he is petulant and lonely. The king's minions suggest that perhaps a harem of the most beautiful young virgins might help him feel better. They will gather the virgins from far and wide. Each night, a different girl will come in to him. Whichever one he likes best will be the new queen. This does soothe the king's damaged ego (imagine that!). Esther, a Jewish orphan raised by her uncle, Mordecai, is one of the girls summoned. Before the young women can enter the king's chamber, however, they must undergo a year-long beautifying regime supervised by eunuchs—a year of sloughing, and moisturizing, and being perfumed—rid of any natural fragrance. The whole thing might be infuriating if it wasn't so over-the-top that it's comical.

A Greek version of Esther has a totally different feel than the Hebrew. (You can find it among the Apocryphal books of the Old Testament as *Additions to Esther*.) In the Greek version there's no comedy. The narrator delivers his grave lesson in a serious tone. The Hebrew version is meant to get you laughing at kings, goyish pomposity, enormous egos.

After the king's eunuchs spend the year moisturizing and perfuming each virgin so that she may be fit to come near the king—when at last she is ready to enter the king's chamber on her given night, if the virgin doesn't "delight" the king, she is never summoned again. But Esther succeeds in delighting the king so much more than all the other virgins that he sets the royal crown upon her head—likely a mix of both beauty and skill. Midrash speaks of Esther as one of the most beautiful women ever created. She remained eternally young, according to legend. When she married the king, so the stories go, she was at least forty years old, possibly even eighty, according to some. I'm not sure that the concept of eternal youth has ever been helpful to anyone, but thinking of Esther as eighty is satisfying somehow—more of a venerable trickster who has seen a lot in her day than someone young and naïve.

Esther's Jewish identity remains hidden from the king. Rabbi Spilker points out that even this is pretty humorous, because her uncle is known as Mordecai-the-Jew. It's all one name—further evidence that the king is more clueless than rakishly desirable. Part of the farce of Esther is seen in a plot that is improbable. Though Mordecai is known as Mordecai-the-Jew, no one knows that his cousin Esther is Jewish. Farce works off some of these irrational or unreasonable elements.

Men Behaving Badly

After Esther is in place in the palace, we meet the evil villain: Haman. The king is a sort of ineffectual buffoon. Haman's a treacherous buffoon—though, in keeping with farce, he's more laughable than scary. He's a prince in the king's court who, for no apparent reason, is suddenly given the highest place in the kingdom. The king commands everyone to bow down to Haman wherever he goes, and most people do it—but Mordecai refuses to bow down. This may seem brave and honorable until you realize his refusal to bow down ends up endangering the entire Jewish community. Haman is so angry that he decides not only to kill Mordecai, but also to annihilate every Jew that lives on the face of the earth. Though Mordecai's refusal to bow to Haman is often explained as if it displays loyalty to the Jewish law, Rabbi Spilker points out, Jews bow down to humans many times in the Torah. "Why," he asks, "to save all the Jews from perishing, couldn't Mordecai have bowed down just a little?"

Rabbi Spilker keeps posing questions and saying, "These are questions. I'm not answering them." The Greek version of the story seems to anticipate the questions and tries to dispel them immediately. Lest anyone see Mordecai as yet another ego-driven man behaving badly, he prays to God (whose name is never mentioned in the canonical version): "You know all things; you know O Lord, that it was not in insolence or pride or for any love of glory that I did this, and refused to bow down to this proud Haman, for I would have been willing to kiss the soles of his feet to save Israel! But I did this so that I might not set human glory above the glory of God." Was someone possibly trying to do a little whitewashing here?

Haman casts lots (*pur* is the Persian word) to decide the day for the slaughter—the die lands on the thirteenth day of the month of Adar. Once the date is decided in this game of chance, Haman goes to the king to convince him of the plan. He tells the king there are strange people scattered among "our people" who have strange ways—they don't honor the laws of the empire. It doesn't profit the king to tolerate them. Let them all be destroyed. The king agrees without much thought and sends out a decree "to destroy, to slay, and to annihilate all Jews, young and old, women and children, in one day, the thirteenth day of the twelfth month."

That the king casually agrees to this is ludicrous. Rabbi Cabelli wrote in his e-mail, "The story of Haman's desire to kill all the Jews, because of his indignation at not being able to shame Mordecai, is a perfect parallel to the King's desire to put all the women in their place, because of his indignation at not being able to shame Vashti." The parallelism in language and content are unmistakable.

These parallels underscore how foolish the men are. Cabelli says, "One cannot fully appreciate the story of how foolishly tyrants behave and the threat that this poses to Jews, without seeing its context in how tyrants tyrannize, always, inevitably, those who are vulnerable—Jews as the quintessential 'other,' women as 'women' in a patriarchal, androcentric society. And if you stay silent while one is oppressed, the door is opened to acquiescence when others are similarly attacked." A timeless tale, indeed.

Mordecai learns of the king's decree and sends an urgent message to Esther, asking for her help. She must speak to the king. He didn't bow down to Haman and now all their people are about to be annihilated!

You could say that Mordecai has created a crisis that he can't solve himself. So he goes to the woman for help. This happens.

Who Knows?

Esther is initially reluctant to do what Mordecai asks because if you go to the king's chamber without being summoned you are put to death. The only chance you have is if the king holds out his "golden scepter" toward you. Esther tells Mordecai that the king hasn't summoned her to his chamber for a whole month, so the "golden scepter" may not be likely to point in her direction. The euphemistic nature of the golden scepter is pretty obvious. The bawdy humor sets a comic, rather than tragic, tone. We also see how unpredictable the situation is for Esther.

Mordecai convinces Esther to give it a try, not by offering her an infallible directive from God, but by posing a question: Who knows? Maybe you're in this place at this time for a reason. God is not flashy or obvious in the book of Esther. In fact, God is not mentioned at all. Nothing is certain—ambiguity prevails—but Esther decides to act to divert the coming disaster. She decides, "If I perish, I perish."

It may actually be the absence of God that makes Esther a compelling book for our times. No prophet hears God's voice. God has no instructions or directions or appearances. If God is present, God is hidden. The book of Esther takes place after the major events in biblical history. God doesn't show up in a pillar of fire or at the door of Moses's tent. God's not handing people tablets or revealing an obvious path. This sounds familiar. We may say we hear God's voice in Scripture, or our neighbor, or the poor, but that's a little different than hearing a voice from heaven. Faith includes ambiguity and mystery. Rabbi Spilker says the story of Esther is about having faith in a time when it is not easy to have faith. God is not apparent, but Mordecai urges Esther not "to keep silence at such a time as this."

So Esther, who so far has seemed a little like a beauty queen—fine to be intimate with the power if the power chooses her, reveals another side of her personality. Her beauty makes her desirable to the powers-that-be, but this doesn't mean she has to give in to them. Without guarantees of any kind, she decides to act—to risk her life for her people. The path to salvation in this instance involves something different than puritanical immaculacy.

It may actually be the absence of God that makes Esther a compelling book for our times. No prophet hears God's voice. God has no instructions or directions or appearances. If God is present, God is hidden. Faith includes ambiguity and mystery.

Esther goes to the king's chamber. The golden scepter points in her direction. In fact, she pleases the king so immensely that he says he will do anything she asks. She asks him to come to dinner and bring Haman along. They drink wine. The king is happy. He tells Esther to ask whatever she wants of him. She asks him to come to dinner with Haman again the next evening. Haman, ever the clueless egomaniac, goes home and regales his household with stories of his great success in court, his general splendor and riches—how he, and only he, has been invited to dine with Esther and the king.

At dinner the next evening, Esther tells the king of the terrible plan to be carried out against her people. The king seems astonished. How has this come about? Who is the man? (Of course the king himself has been more than a little involved, but this somehow escapes him.) Esther says, he is right here! And she points at Haman: it's the wicked Haman. The king rises in wrath from the table and goes into the garden. Meanwhile, Haman throws himself on the couch where Esther is reclining to plead for mercy. When the king comes back in, he sees Haman near Esther and cries, "Will he even assault the queen in my presence, in my own house?" It's a classic sort of humorous misinterpretation. One of the eunuchs suggests that they take Haman to the preposterously large gallows he had been constructing for Mordecai—as high as a six-story building—and hang Haman in Mordecai's place.

The king gives Mordecai Haman's house and his place in court, and the king issues another decree—because for some reason he can't just call it off. He has to issue a decree to undo the first decree calling for annihilation. On that day the Jews were to be slaughtered, they instead will defend themselves. And they do, perhaps a tad too robustly.

Rabbi Spilker notes that the challenge in reading about the violence done in retaliation by the Jews is not in the preemptive strike the Jews mount against the Persians, because (according to the story) the king can't revoke a decree once he's put it out there, so of course the only way they can save themselves is to fight. The challenge is in the fact that Esther asks for an extra day to slay more people. He recalls an incident in 1994 when an American Israeli massacred thirty-six Palestinians at the cave of the patriarchs after hearing Esther read. He says, of course, we must teach against this sort of reading.

He says it might help to think of the violence done by the Jewish people in Esther more in the vein of the movie *The Inglorious Bastards*—a reimagining where, instead of being victims, a Jewish squad of Nazi-hunters beat up the Nazis and eventually kill Hitler and end World War II. Esther is a story that never happened. But it's the sort of story that, if the Cossacks are storming your village, might be helpful to read. It is by no means a story meant to incite violence. It's a farce about an unlikely series of events—a series of ridiculous and irrevocable edicts—in which an insignificant and subservient minority ends up wielding the highest power in the empire. Instead of being annihilated, the Jewish people are saved. The reverse occurs.

Female Jesus

Some Christians speak of Esther as a type of Christ. She's a figure who rises up in the midst of empire to save her people. Sam Wells, vicar of St. Martin-in-the-Fields, London, preached at Duke University's chapel and said, "Esther is a kind of Jesus, at the right hand of God, laying down her life for the salvation of the Jews." Mark Driscoll, coming from a different place, concurs, saying, "Ultimately Esther is a type of Christ." Think of that—a female Jesus. Or could we say, at least say, that as a type of Christ she gives us a glimpse of the feminine face of God? We don't get to see that a lot. But that's the glimpse we get in Esther.

Christians believe in a God who reveals godself, not in the expected way of the gods—all-powerful and mighty, but in a rather unexpected way—as a God who empties godself of power for love, a God who gets a body and dies on the cross. In the midrash Esther prays the words of Psalm 22, "My God, my God why hast thou forsaken me?" That was the same prayer Jesus prayed on the cross, according to the Gospels. This is not a warrior-god armed for battle. Or a stoic, invulnerable, unfeeling god.

Esther is vulnerable as a woman and a Jew in the Persian Empire. She saves her people, not by threatening the foolish king, or frightening him, or challenging him to a fight, but by seducing him. As Sam Wells says, "She can wrap the king around her little finger by using her exquisite sense of timing, her insight into human nature, her beauty and her sexual expertise." Her power comes through the desire she inspires in the king. Maybe she *is* a type of Christ. Maybe this is a revelation of how God works.

The world keeps expecting a violent savior—and has done so pretty much forever, as if violence is necessary to combat the darkness and evil. Obviously the powers believe in violence as a way to solve problems. It's neither very creative nor mature. In Esther, God's people are saved in a story full of laughter and lovemaking. It might help to see God as an inviting lover sometimes instead of a mighty fortress.

We really don't have that many images of God acting *womanish* (as Alice Walker defined it, *like a woman*, usually referring to outrageous, audacious, courageous, or willful behavior—one who loves everyone). Esther as a type of Christ woos, persuades, demurs. Her territory is definitely more a persuasive sort of Eros than a toxic sort of masculinity.

Both Jewish and Christian interpreters have most often concluded that though God is not mentioned in the book, God acts through Esther. God acts through a woman—like a woman.

Reclaiming Eros

Eros isn't necessarily sexual, but it is love *embodied*. It's a kind of desire experienced not just cerebrally, rationally—but wholly—a desire to join with something outside of yourself. It's a creative impulse toward joy.

I remember being surprised to discover that Pope Benedict XVI, in his first papal encyclical, spoke of the urgent need for Christianity to re-embrace Eros. I'm not exactly sure why I was surprised—maybe because hope is surprising.

Passionate desire, Benedict said, is a deeply important part of faith. Cutting off Eros from our definitions of Christian love or godly love impoverishes that love. Eliminating Eros makes godly love seem sterile and disconnected—not the kind of thing you long for "like the deer pants for water." The pope even quoted Nietzsche, who was notoriously suspect of what he saw as a prudish, life-denying, and resentful Christianity. Nietzsche said, "Christianity gave Eros poison to drink: He did not die of it to be sure, but degenerated into a vice." His claim that Christianity didn't get rid of Eros (how could it?) but perverted it is disappointingly accurate. What could the church have been thinking, giving Eros poison to drink?

Maybe desire is notoriously difficult to precisely control, but vilifying it (as the church has been wont to do at times) hasn't made the world a better place.

Eros drives us outside and beyond our selves. Benedict said Eros is the presence of God's life (this very lively life) among us. To desire is to be open to the world, not closed up in some dark basement with the shades pulled. Maybe there's something humbling about desire (for food, for water, for touch), because it is a reminder built into our body and soul that we're dependent on what's other than our selves—we actually need plants, and animals, and air, and other people to survive. We're not self-sufficient. But this dependence is the basis of all relationship—all the loves that make life meaningful and worth living.

Passionate desire is a godly thing. God loves us, likes us, desires us. Passionately. Christian theology made a mistake when it tried to separate Eros from Christian love. You don't see this sort of separation so much in Judaism, which embraces the body and has a far healthier relationship to sensuality. Judaism never suffers as much from the Greek dualism of body and spirit that pervades Christian thought.

Maybe Esther, this very Jewish heroine, can nudge us back toward connecting God's love and Eros again, introducing us to a God more seductive than militaristic, more beautiful than violent. "Beauty will save the world," writes Dostoevsky. Esther, the wielder of Eros, helps us imagine that.

8 Purim
The Farce Awakens

There is a thin line that separates laughter and pain,
comedy and tragedy, humor and hurt.

—Erma Bombeck

On the day the Jews were to be annihilated by the power of the
biggest empire the world had ever known, the small, scrappy
group of exiles defeat their foes emphatically. Mordecai decrees
that for all time from now on, on the anniversary of this day,
the fourteenth day of the month of Adar, the Jewish people will
celebrate with feasting and holidaymaking: "These days should
be remembered and kept throughout every generation, in every family, province, and city and these days of Purim shall
never fall into disuse among the Jews." They will send good
food to each other and give to the poor. They will celebrate
the day on which the Jews got relief from their sadness, when
their sorrow was turned into laughter. The feast day was to be
named after the pur (the lots) that Haman cast. Esther writes
down these happy instructions, fixing the practice of Purim in
perpetuity—come good days and bad. According to the Yivo
Encyclopedia of Jews in Eastern Europe, Purim continued to
be celebrated in the ghettos and concentration camps during
World War II, when hope must have surely seemed far-flung.

Some scholars have surmised that Jews in the diaspora would have been celebrating the spring festivals of the cultures in which they found themselves when the book of Esther was written. Since Esther's name is a derivative of Ishtar, and Mordecai, Marduk (popular characters in Babylonian mythology), it's possible that the book of Esther and the celebration it institutes were ingenious ways for the Jewish people to claim these ancient characters and seasonal celebration as their own.

The celebration has features common among other peoples, religions, and civilizations. As Rabbi Spilker noted, it has a lot in common with Mardi Gras and other antinomian holidays, where the law of the status quo is overthrown for a day.

In the spirit of the book of Esther, Purim is a funny holiday. Esther is read aloud in the synagogue, and whenever Haman's name is mentioned (which is fifty-four times) everyone rattles special noisemakers made for the occasion. Some people write Haman's name on the bottom of their shoe and stamp their feet to blot out his name as instructed by the ancient rabbis, who often have a sense of humor.

The feast includes special foods —little triangle-shaped pastries filled with poppy seeds, chocolate, or apricot called Hamantaschen—Haman's pockets, or Haman's hat. Italian Jews enjoy pastries called Orecchie di Aman—Haman's ears—flavored with lemon rind, vanilla, and rum. Moroccan Jews bake special challah bread in the shape of Haman's head called the eyes of Haman. The eyes are made of boiled eggs.

The most important obligations of the day are to eat a festive meal and be happy. What great obligations. And not only eat and be happy, but drink wine, lots of it. The sages of the ancient Talmud said that people should drink so much wine on Purim that they can no longer distinguish between the phrases "cursed is Haman" and "blessed is Mordecai." Later, some rabbis said, maybe after all, you should only drink a little more than usual—but, still, you are obliged to drink, laugh, and have fun.

Rabbi Spilker talked about the parade held in Tel Aviv every year called "Adloyada" or *until one no longer knows*—the rabbinical measure of how drunk you should get. There are DJs and street dances and giant floats. The pictures I found on the Internet show people in Guy Fawkes masks, dance troupes, and loads of women in fishnet stockings, high heels, micro-mini hot pants, and sexy push-up bustiers.

The tradition of dressing up in costumes for Purim is explained in a variety of ways. One is that Purim represents "the hidden." Esther keeps her Jewish identity hidden, and God is masked in the book of Esther. People dress up to emulate God, who disguised God's presence but who was nevertheless among them. Or the tradition may stem from spring masquerade festivals that the Jews adopted for their own merriment.

The carnival-like atmosphere of the festival of Purim certainly contributes to a humorous reading of the book. The existential threat seems to build just so the audience can watch with delight and laugh with relief when it is overcome.

Rabbi Alan Shavit-Lonstein, the Genius at the Apple Store, told me that even the most serious, conservative, traditional Jews bring out the humor in the book of Esther at Purim. He remembered a friend who lost her life in a suicide bus attack in Israel. He said she had never been given to humor, but as she read the Esther scroll on Purim, when it came to the part where Esther takes off her clothes, she started taking off her clothes. She had layers on underneath, but still, it was funny in a risqué sort of way.

When Rabbi Shavit-Lonstein was studying in a very traditional school in Israel, where you are expected to always show great respect for your teachers, Purim was the one day you could question them—the day you didn't have to show honor to them in the same way you did all the other days. Even at the most traditional yeshivot, the rabbis allowed men to dress as women on this day—something usually forbidden. Students cross-dressed with clothing borrowed from their mothers and sisters. Hebrew and Yiddish newspapers often printed special editions for the day, including parody and satirical critiques of local and world politics.

The subversive character of the holiday is embodied in the Purim spiel, a play that reenacts the biblical story in a way that often satirizes current events.

In an NPR interview, Nahma Sandrow, a historian of Yiddish theater, said, Purim "juxtaposes the sacred and profane." Over the centuries the Purim spiel has given players "license to make fun of the ruling class. The king is the local lord of whatever time and place the play is being put on." Deborah Eisenbach-Budner, the education director at Portland's Havurah Shalom congregation, adds, "The Purim spiel is so much about power. There's no way to get around that. It's about power, and lack of power, and vulnerability. So that translates into politics . . . it's so much about resistance." Laughing at kings is a way of not giving the powerful the power they so pompously claim.

Such laughter also gives us room to breathe—freeing us from paralysis when we feel caught in a hopeless place. The way some of us might feel an immense sense of relief (relief almost seems to be the best word for it) when we watch Alec Baldwin playing Donald Trump on *Saturday Night Live*. Laughter does something for us that we desperately need, even (or maybe especially) in the most serious circumstances.

Today We Will Merry Merry Be

My first experience of Purim is at the Beth Jacob Congregation south of St. Paul. They are going with a Star Wars theme: The Farce Awakens. The video promoting it on their website makes me laugh.

As soon as I confirm people from outside the congregation are welcome at the celebration, I convince my colleague, the Rev. Russell, to go with me. Rabbi Morris Allen told me that I should definitely wear a costume if I want to get into the spirit of things. I've never really enjoyed costumes, but I buy a poncho at Target and wear a straw hat, hoping to approximate a llama farmer. When I pick up Russell, he has on a long bathrobe and a scarf wrapped around his head. He said he was going for a Jedi look. He is great with costumes. When we arrive at the synagogue, hardly any cars have appeared in the parking lot, so we decide to sit there for a while. People start arriving slowly. Russell keeps saying, "That person isn't wearing a costume." Or, "The little boy is the only one dressed up." As more cars show up and Russell is increasingly convinced no one is wearing a costume, he starts having a panic attack—decides he looks more like a suicide bomber than a Star Wars character and refuses to go in. I get out and tell him to go ahead and take the car back to his house so he can change his clothes.

I'm greeted by Rabbi Allen, I presume, though it's difficult to tell through his Darth Vader mask. He is on rollerblades, carrying a light saber. I feel a little lost and unsure what to do until Vicky, an older woman wearing a yarmulke but no costume, kindly introduces herself to me and gives me the rundown. She helps me get a noisemaker, called a gragger. Some graggers are wooden; some are Kraft Macaroni and Cheese boxes decorated with children's renditions of the evil Haman. Mine features Haman with an eye patch and fangs. Vicky is new to Beth Jacob. She has just moved to Minnesota from Seattle. I'm happy to be able to sit with someone else who is slightly uncomfortable.

I tell her I'm a pastor from a Lutheran congregation. She says she doesn't know much about Christianity and asks me what beliefs we share. This question makes me nervous. Do I say, "Well, actually, we got everything from you and tried to make it about us," or do I talk about love, and grace, and justice? Or is she just testing me to see if I can handle it? More than anything, I feel like apologizing—for supersessionism, and Martin Luther, and Paul, and the Inquisition, and the Holocaust. I end up evading the question and talk about how much I've learned from rabbinic modes of interpretation—how I wished I'd learned more about them in seminary. I ask if she knows Avivah Zornberg's work. She said she

> *I tell her I'm a pastor from a Lutheran congregation. She says she doesn't know much about Christianity and asks me what beliefs we share. This question makes me nervous. More than anything, I feel like apologizing—for supersessionism, and Martin Luther, and Paul, and the Inquisition, and the Holocaust.*

did and told me about a therapist-rabbi she knew in Seattle who used similar psychoanalytic categories to interpret Torah as a sort of inner spirituality. He spoke about the human compulsion toward idolatry—how we keep making gods and never get it right. I'm so glad she's led the conversation here—we share a belief in a God much larger (or smaller, or different) than the idols to which we cling. That's what I should have said.

Bunches of helium balloons bearing images of the Millennium Falcon decorate the sanctuary. The person in front of me is wearing a voluminous black wig. Across the aisle a woman is dressed in a blue suit and a flesh colored swim cap with a few cotton balls glued to the side and stretched out to approximate unkempt white hair. She is carrying a sign that says "Vote Mordecai Sanders" on one side and "Haters? Get rid of them" on the other. She's with a woman wearing an orange wig topped with a Make America Great cap. Her sign says "Vote Haman J. Trump" on one side and "Jews Are Losers" on the other.

Two children dressed as a jagaroo (jaguar plus kangaroo) walk up and down the aisles. One is the head, the other the tail. It's not the most convincing costume, but I'm impressed with the elaborate poster they carry explaining the diet, digestive system, and habitat of the jagaroo.

The service begins informally with the singing of traditional Purim songs. The first few are in Hebrew, which I can't understand, but I like, *Oh Once There Was a Wicked, Wicked Man*, a folk tune that goes like this:

Oh once there was a wicked wicked man,
And Haman was his name.
He would have murdered all the Jews,
Though they were not to blame.

CHORUS:
Oh today we'll merry merry be
Oh today we'll merry merry be
Oh today we'll merry merry be
And nosh some hamentashen.

And Esther was a lovely queen
Of King Ahashveyrosh
When Haman said he'd kill us all,
Oh my how he did scare us.

CHORUS:
Oh today we'll merry merry be
Oh today we'll merry merry be
Oh today we'll merry merry be
And nosh some hamentashen.

In spite of Haman's awful plan
And the scare he gave us
Esther was so brave and strong
She knew just how to save us.

CHORUS:
Oh today we'll merry merry be
Oh today we'll merry merry be
Oh today we'll merry merry be
And nosh some hamentashen.

So Haman got his just desserts
And we had won the day
And Esther we will ne'er forget

And on this day we say:
Oh today we'll merry merry be
Oh today we'll merry merry be
Oh today we'll merry merry be
And nosh some hamentashen.

An older man dressed as Raggedy Andy and his wife, per-haps, dressed as Raggedy Ann make their way to the front of the sanctuary. We are going to practice for the Megillah (the scroll of Esther) reading. When they hold up the "go" sign, we are to rattle our noisemakers. When they hold up the "stop" sign, we stop.

Various cantors take turns chanting the Megillah. The jux-taposition of the sacred and the profane is flagrant—like the serious, ancient-looking scroll in the arms of a man dressed as a rabbit with long bunny ears hanging down to his waist and a fuzzy tail attached to his bottom. A woman wearing a football uniform sings the Hebrew beautifully and then sud-denly switches to a high-pitched, whiny nasal voice in the middle of chapter three. I never imagined you could chant in Hebrew and do a funny voice at the same time. I know she's trying to do a Haman voice, even though I can't understand the Hebrew, because Raggedy Ann and Andy flip their signs to "Go!" We rattle our noisemakers.

Somewhere around chapter five or six (I'm not sure be-cause I can't quite follow what's happening), everyone gets up to parade around the sanctuary. Foxes, cats, Batman, Yoda, yellow Minions, and twenty little girls dressed as Esther shimmy down the aisle to a sort-of New Orleans jazz beat. A pregnant woman in a witch's hat holds the hand of a boy dressed as a dragon.

After the parade we go back to the reading, just for a bit, until some teenage boys disrupt it. One's wearing a mask like the bad guys in Mad Max. There's some sort of staged kerfuffle after which they yell, "The Megillah has been kidnapped and must be freed" with the ransom they will be collecting in the baskets they are passing up and down the aisles. It's a ruse. They are collecting the money for a social service agency that provides shelter for homeless teens.

People have been talking and getting up and walking around throughout the whole service, so I'm not really sure whether or not it's over until Vicki stands up and moves toward the aisle. She turns back to grab my hand in hers and invites me to stay for the party. She quickly disappears in the crowd leaving the sanctuary, and I don't see her again. I go stand by the bathrooms and call Russell. I tell him that, in fact, nearly everyone is in costume and now he may feel uncomfortable without one but he really should come in and join me for the party.

I hang out by the Hamantaschen to wait for him. Though I saw recipes online for Pareve Cinnamon Dulce de Leche Hamantaschen, Cardamom-Scented Hamantaschen with Pear and Goat Cheese Filling, S'more and Nutella Hamantaschen, at Beth Jacob, Haman's pockets are all filled with the more traditional poppy seed, apricot, and raspberry filling. I choose the poppy seed, which turns out to be a little bland when you have pear and goat cheese on the mind.

A DJ and strobe lights entertain us. Quite a few people dance. Tables full of various treats—chocolate, and pretzels, and popcorn balls, and deviled eggs with special Star Wars names—line the perimeters of the room. Someone's selling a novel about Esther.

I meet Russell at the table with the alcohol. There's lots of beer and two big, glass dispensers full of neon-colored liquid, one labeled Jedi Juice, the other, Yoda Soda. I ask the man standing behind the table what they are. He says the green one is gin, the blue one, vodka. I have a few sips of the (very sweet) green one and toss it. Russell has three glasses of blue Jedi Juice.

As I was scanning the Internet for Purim celebrations, I saw there was a Twin Cities–wide Purim after-party in 2013 called Cirque Du Purim, which featured fire jugglers, stilt walkers, and DJ Becca Gee "spinning sick beats." This year the same organization is throwing another party, and the invitation says, "Yes, we know it's a weeknight. Yes, we know it's late. But it's Purim, people! This only happens once a year! It's your religious OBLIGATION to party like it's 5776."

Russell and I leave the synagogue after-party for the city-wide after-party where we've arranged to meet another pastor-friend, John. When we walk in the bar, we see no fire jugglers. I can tell immediately that we are outside the intended age demographic. It's obviously a mixer for young people, but we go ahead and fill out a brief survey and get two drink tickets each and a wristband.

Russell and John and I eventually make our way to a booth. Pretty much everyone ignores us, but not at all in a mean way. I feel awkward but merry. I think how great it is to have a religious obligation "to have a festive meal and be happy." I've fulfilled that mitzvah at least.

Not Throwing Away Her Shot: A Pointed Purim Spiel

After my first Purim, I look forward to the next. This year Mt.
Zion, a Reform Synagogue near our church, is putting on a
Hamilton-themed Purim spiel. It's the promise of a satirical
Jewish take on *Hamilton* that brings me to the Esther study
with Rabbi Spilker, where I meet the old man and drink the
Sam Adams. Some ingenious mind (Cantor Jamie Marx) has
somehow managed to rewrite the words to all the *Hamilton*
songs to reflect Esther's story. There's a teaser on the website
introducing the cast at Mt. Zion and the first song. The chorus sings, "Does the world celebrate her name? What's your
name, Miss?" And a teenager with a great voice steps up and
sings, "Esther Niece of Mordecai. My name is Esther Niece of
Mordecai and my story isn't nearly done. Just you wait. Just
you wait." I can hardly wait.

I saw *Hamilton* recently in Chicago, and even though I was
a little resistant to all the mania (Olivia already had the sound
track memorized), l loved it. In the Purim version, Esther (a
girl) is the Hamilton figure. She is "young, clever, and Jewish"
and she's not throwing away her shot.

After the book study, we move to an open space outside
the sanctuary to await the spiel. A man dressed as a pirate (as
far as I can tell) moves through the crowd offering people a
smell of the small sachet he holds up. I'm eager to take him
up on it when he gets to me, though I have no idea what it's
all about. It smells of cloves and cinnamon. Later I read on
the Internet that Purim is a holiday that rouses the senses,
with bright costumes and food, but the one sense often un-
accounted for is smell, which is probably the one sense most
fitting for Esther. Both Mordecai and Esther are compared to

scents. Midrash interprets Mordecai's name as *pure myrrh*. Esther's Hebrew name, Hadassah, means myrtle, a flowering tree known for its fragrance. Myrtle is sacred to the goddess of love, Aphrodite.

More significantly, perhaps, just as God is said to be present in the story though we can't see God or hear God, so we are aware of scent though we can't see or hear it. God is ever-present though hidden from our view: God is present as scent. The metaphor may not seem fitting on every occasion (walking through the subway or when riding in a small car with a dog and the windows rolled up), but I am grateful for the sensuality of the Jewish tradition—to be shown that we might know God through our sense of smell—our noses—something so other than our vision, or our ears, or our intellect.

I'm eager when it comes time to enter the sanctuary and hear the Megillah reading, followed by Lin-Manuel Miranda's rousing rap revised to fit a Jewish resistance story. At Mt. Zion the audience participation is slightly different than at Beth Jacob. We practice yelling "Boo" when Haman is mentioned. "Whoo HOOH" is our response to Vashti. Whenever we hear Esther's name, we are to yell, "You Go Girl!"

After the reading, the lights are dimmed, and the players take the stage. I'm somehow both delighted and moved by the first glimpse of the king. He is a high school kid doing a very good impression of Donald Trump while rapping Jewish lyrics to a Hamilton song with perfect beat. And a good voice. It's spot on, hilarious, brilliant.

I don't think anyone, even Trump's greatest fans, could read Esther in the Trump era and not see parallels. And I'm not sure Trump would object to the parallels—the king is very, very rich and famous, and this gives him all the access he wants to the ladies. Through another lens, the king is a pompous, childish man with power—dependent on his advisors, who are all around him (including an anti-Semitic advisor) directing his every move.

After calling for Vashti to come parade in front of his drunken party, Trump/the king/the teenage boy says, "No one respects women more than I do. Now shut up and dance," all the while barely taking his eyes off his cell phone.

When Haman is proposing the edict that will enforce the murder of every Jew, Trump/the king/the teenage boy, who is busy texting, says without looking up, "Do I need to know the details?" It definitely reads as a funny moment, not a tragic one. Everyone in the audience laughs.

The NPR interview I had heard earlier predicted, "Purim spiels across the country tonight will feature kings who fire off angry tweets. It's pointed humor," but Eisenbach-Budner says, "That's the Purim spiels's job."

Amidst farcical, terrible, and unprecedented events, who knows? Maybe you are here at such a time as this for a reason.

The spiel at Mt. Zion ends with a rousing chorus. "Everyone must stand up tall and true. Consider the words you say cuz history has its eyes on you."

"There is a thin line that separates laughter and pain, comedy and tragedy, humor and hurt," as Erma Bombeck once said. Or as my friend Abigail Pelham puts it, "Tragedy proclaims the grandeur of humankind. Comedy tells us the grandeur is a sham." Amidst farcical, terrible, and unprecedented events, who knows? Maybe you are here at such a time as this for a reason.

9 Shoah

Scapegoating and Status-Seeking

Teach your tongue to say, "I don't know," lest you be
exposed as a liar.

—The Talmud

I was born when all I once
feared—I could
love.

—Rab'ia al Basr

In the Hebrew Scripture, the people of God are enslaved, oppressed by one empire after another, and persecuted when
they refuse to accommodate to the empire's ways. Daniel is
thrown in the lion's den for his refusal to assimilate. "He was
there for six days," we read in the Apocrypha. "There were
seven lions in the den and every day they had been given
two human bodies and two sheep, but now they were given
nothing, so that they would devour Daniel."

In the stories of the Maccabees, Antiochus, the ruler of
the Seleucid Empire, defiles the Jewish sanctuaries, makes
the possession of Torah a capital offense, bans Sabbaths,
religious feasts, and circumcision. The Jewish people are
made vassals of Rome and, again, when they will not ac-

commodate to the empire, their sanctuaries are destroyed, their people killed, forced into slavery, or compelled to flee from their homes.

The story of the Jewish people in Scripture is a story of a displaced people who long for a home where they might finally be safe. The tension is a historical tragedy, but in Scripture it is also an existential plight. One of the important things that becomes clear in midrashic literature is that to be the people of God is in some sense to be unsettled. The history of the people of God is torturous and joyous—it is not easy or simple. Faith is not a set of answers you can write down on a sheet of paper—to be the people of God is to struggle.

At the ritual Passover Seder meal, the youngest child in a family is obliged to ask four traditional questions, which represent four attitudes toward the narratives of redemption, according to Avivah Zornberg. The attitudes are those of the wise son, who knows the question and asks it; the wicked son, who knows the question but refuses to ask it; the simple son, who knows the question but is indifferent to it; and the ignorant son, who doesn't know the question so can't ask it. So the Jewish child's first expression of faith, according to Zornberg, is not a statement of belief, but the first genuinely expressed question. According to the midrashic sensibilities, questions propel the narratives of faith to keep having meaning for the generations.

The Christian tradition has often been more oriented toward answers. It is not uncommon to hear Christians say, "Jesus is the answer." But like the Jewish rabbis, Jesus asks more questions than he answers. "Who do you say that I am?" "What is it you want?" "Why are you so afraid?" "Why do you look at the speck of sawdust in your brother's eye and pay no attention to your own?" On the cross Jesus cries, "My God, My God, why have you forsaken me?"

Unlike most narratives of nations we encounter in history, the Jewish narratives in the Hebrew Bible are self-critical.

The Christian tradition has often been more oriented toward answers. It is not uncommon to hear Christians say, "Jesus is the answer." But like the Jewish rabbis, Jesus asks more questions than he answers. "Who do you say that I am?" "What is it you want?" "Why are you so afraid?"

Instead of placing the blame for the nation's struggles on an outside force (some *other* people, a scapegoat) the editors who revise the old stories to compose the official history looked internally—to the nation's own sins. The problem wasn't just the Assyrians or the Babylonians. The problem was that the people of Israel did not trust in the God who loved them and freed them. As in the rest of Scripture, the editors' concerns were not merely to record historical fact, but convey a more profound truth, a truth that is revelatory even now.

Sadly as the editors focus on the idolatry, they zoom in on the feminine face of God. Instead of celebrating the mother as one more expression of the unfathomably loving God of Israel, she is portrayed as a threat—as the source of idolatry. (One might even say that she becomes the scapegoat here.)

I can see how the story ends up being framed this way. I'm also grieved that we lose so much of the laboring, breasted, womanly expression of God.

The stories of Israel are the stories of a people who are compelled by God and prophets to acknowledge their faults—

their lack of trust and love. They are not triumphal stories. They are stories of struggle. But though a certain existential unsettledness is very much a part of the faith of the people of God, there is also the very catastrophic historical reality of what happens to a people who are driven from their land, marginalized, and demeaned.

Christianity Has a Shameful History of Anti-Semitism

Although there is much humor in Esther, one rabbi warned that Esther and Purim have an underlying message that is so serious it may get lost in the Hamilton-esque romps. It is a story of a people who have, in fact, been subject to genocide. In the book of Esther, a man with power means to kill all Jews and make that genocide into law. We must attend to the fact that this actually happened in Germany in the twentieth century. It is something that people have actually experienced. Perhaps if Esther was not so system-atically ignored in Christianity, the story of Haman could have deterred the church from its persistent descents into anti-Semitism.

Though the Christian faith, obviously, came from Judaism and owes its life to it, Christianity has a long and shameful history of anti-Semitism. You can see a growing combative-ness toward Jewish people who do not accept Jesus as the Messiah almost right off the bat. If you read the book of Acts as a Christian, it's a story of how the gospel spread. If you read it as a Jewish person, well, by chapter 3, Peter is accusing the men of Israel of murdering the author of life. It's the beginning of the Christians' using the Jewish Scripture against the Jewish people. As The Way spreads, so does animosity toward the Jewish people who don't accept it.

After World War II and the horrors of the Holocaust, Christianity became much more aware of the problems with supersessionsim, reading our texts as if they are meant to supersede Judaism, but the damage can't be undone.

Watching *Shoah* and Reading the New Testament

I had been watching the film *Shoah* for weeks when Matthew 23:1–12 came up in the lectionary:

> Then Jesus said to the crowds and to his disciples, "The scribes and the Pharisees sit on Moses' seat; therefore, do whatever they teach you and follow it; but do not do as they do, for they do not practice what they teach. They tie up heavy burdens, hard to bear, and lay them on the shoulders of others; but they themselves are unwilling to lift a finger to move them. They do all their deeds to be seen by others; for they make their phylacteries broad and their fringes long. They love to have the place of honor at banquets and the best seats in the synagogues, and to be greeted with respect in the marketplaces, and to have people call them rabbi. But you are not to be called rabbi, for you have one teacher, and you are all students. And call no one your father on earth, for you have one Father—the one in heaven. Nor are you to be called instructors, for you have one instructor, the Messiah. The greatest among you will be your servant. All who exalt themselves will be humbled, and all who humble themselves will be exalted. (NRSV)

In the context of what I had been watching day after day, in bits and pieces, I could barely bring myself to look at the passage. I had to try to remember that not everybody at church (in fact, probably, nobody but me) happened to be in the middle of watching a nine-and-a-half-hour French documentary about the systematic attempt to exterminate the Jews in Europe. It had been affecting my interpretation of a lot of things. If anyone in my house complained about anything, or if I began to worry that my hair was thinning or that our cat had diabetes, I'd think, "You're not a Jewish person in the Warsaw ghetto in 1942. Have some perspective, for God's sake."

It's a sparse movie, *Shoah*, and—this probably won't come as a surprise—depressing. When it came out in 1985, after eleven years in the making, people called it an incomparable masterpiece. There's no music. No voice-overs. No photos or archival footage—just a Frenchman, wearing bell bottoms and sideburns, asking questions of Jewish survivors, Polish witnesses, and German perpetrators. They answer in Polish, Yiddish, Italian, Hebrew, German, French, and English. Everyone smokes. It was the seventies.

At one point, Claude Lanzmann, the director, is talking to a Jewish man, not a survivor, but a historian—who points out that there was nothing really new about what happened in the beginning. The church had been scapegoating Jewish people for centuries, isolating them in ghettos, stripping them of their rights. He particularly points to Martin Luther (as in the founder of the church in which I am ordained).

In Luther's infamous anti-Semitic treatise, "On the Jews and Their Lies," he describes Jewish people as a "base, whoring people, full of the devil's feces . . . which they wallow in like swine." He calls the synagogue an "incorrigible whore" and an "evil slut." He argues that Jewish synagogues and schools should be set on fire, rabbis be forbidden to preach, books burned, homes razed, property and money confiscated. He says "they" should be shown no mercy or kindness, be afforded no legal protection; the "poisonous envenomed worms" should be drafted into forced labor or expelled for all time. He also seems to advocate their murder, writing, "We are at fault in not slaying them."

Luther regularly uses violent and vulgar language about a lot of people, but there's no question that his anti-Semitism had a considerable effect on Western Christianity. Hitler made good use of this treatise. What if Luther had not been such an enemy to Esther? Might he have recognized a bit of Haman in himself and recanted his terrible words?

Anti-Jewish sentiment among Christians has unleashed an enormous amount of violence throughout history. Watching *Shoah* was making me hyperaware of this when the Matthew passage came up—where Jesus (someone I generally trust and believe in) begins this sort of violent diatribe against the Jewish leaders. It made me feel sick. Surely, if Jesus knew this sort of thing would lead to murderous prejudice, he would have been more graceful.

We could blame what comes across as anti-Jewish sentiment on Matthew, the author of the Gospel. Jesus never would have seen himself as separate from the Jewish community. He's a Jewish teacher. But as Christianity separated from its roots, conflicts arose. Matthew definitely shaped Jesus's words to try to deal with the conflict his community was having with the Jewish leaders years after Jesus died. I mean, I sort of get it—there's conflict, feelings are running high, and you're trying to promote the vision of your community—but do you trash-talk your opponents and make them into caricatures?

We've all been seeing a lot of this sort of behavior on the Internet—divisive rants, everybody speaking disparagingly of the people they don't agree with. But this is the Bible, not political propaganda, and it's disappointing—sort of heart-breaking—to hear Jesus take a mocking tone: "They make their phylacteries broad and their fringes long, . . . and [love] to have people call them rabbi."

It seems like a sort of cheap criticism really—like making fun of people for what they wear. What's wrong with phylacteries? You take a little leather box, and you roll up a piece of parchment with words from Scripture written on it: "You shall love the Lord your God with all your heart and all your soul and all your mind," and you put the piece of parchment in the box, and you fasten it on your hand or your head to remind you that these words shall be in your heart—they shall be a frontlet between the eyes and a token on your hand. I mean, yes, it might look a little odd to wear a small box on your forehead or your hand—but what about that instead of smartphones fastened to our hands and heads—to remind us of the forces that guide us?

The fringes were like tassels that hung from the four corners of a garment so that when you walked, you would feel them brush your skin and see them swing—so you'd remember to delight in God's will and walk in God's way by loving your neighbor and being grateful for creation. That's not exactly like wearing a three-hundred-thousand-dollar dress made from the skin of some endangered animal. As far as trying to exalt yourself goes—these practices Jesus names just don't really seem very offensive.

You don't get truly accurate information about a group by reading the literature of their opponents, obviously. The rants against the Pharisees in Matthew reflect conflict between Jewish people who followed Jesus and those who did not. When Matthew wrote, both groups were trying to figure out how to proceed—how to have faith after the Jewish temple had been destroyed by the Roman Empire.

You can see the conflict all over the New Testament—like there were these different possibilities: one way eventually ends up as Christianity, another way—rabbinic Judaism. Watching these possibilities play out over the centuries, you can see some great and some not-so-great things about where these paths go over time.

The rabbis brought to life the belief that God was present outside of the temple—present even in the smallest details of life. To cultivate an awareness of this presence, you even became attentive to mundane activities—like washing your hands. These weren't heavy burdens, elaborate rituals, to keep people out but simple things to bring God's presence into every moment of the day. God was present in the preparation of a meal, while you worked in the garden, in all the ordinary details of life—God was as present in the kitchen as God was ever-present in the temple. The rabbis believed that you expressed your faith in God through acts of loving-kindness, especially to the poor. Their practices weren't meant to enforce rigidity, but to enable life, though Christian texts often emphasize the legalism.

The midrash is wild and playful—for the rabbis it was a way of "seeking God in their midst," not a way to find some sort of static, rigid, singular answer or formula for living. Questions, for the rabbis, are more important than the answers. I hope someday to learn to read with the imagination that the spirit of rabbinic inquiry embodies.

There's a lot to sort through when you're reading an ancient text—a lot of stuff we don't exactly have access to. But if we use the Bible to condemn people and exalt ourselves, our nation, or our religious practice—if we use it to fuel hatred and prejudice and self-righteousness—it's not a text with much redemptive potential.

You'd think the stories of Hagar, the outsider who is given God's blessing, and the stories that break down the lines between us and them, the whole tenor of the book that witnesses to the living God, who wants to draw all people to her bosom, would help us love each other.

> *The midrash is wild and playful—for the rabbis it was a way of "seeking God in their midst." Questions, for the rabbis, are more important than the answers. I hope someday to learn to read with the imagination that the spirit of rabbinic inquiry embodies.*

How we read our text matters in very real ways. How do we read the New Testament or Matthew 23 in a way that doesn't contribute to the destruction of the world and murderous prejudice?

It doesn't seem that hard, really. A lot of people point out that Jesus isn't actually talking to the Jewish leaders in this text, he's talking to his disciples and the crowds—so he's using indirect communication: he's speaking of the Pharisees but what he's really doing is warning his followers about power and wanting to have power, about seeking status. In some ways Jesus's point is not that different from what you get in Esther.

Maybe people are even, unconsciously, pulled to read these sorts of warnings against status-seeking self-importance as if they are directed at some other—because we've failed so miserably to heed the warning ourselves.

Jesus is pretty serious about calling people to renounce the quest for power, and wealth, and status—to form a community that is antithetical to most of what the empire holds to be important, a community where the poor and the broken, and the weak, and the humble have precedence—come first.

It's beautiful and kind of outrageous. I mean, look at the world in which we live. Can it renounce the quest for status? If there weren't status-seeking creatures to innovate, create jobs, govern us, provide entertainment, improve the economy—wouldn't the world as we know it fall apart?

But Jesus calls into question the status-seeking creature. Although we might have heard of such questions and even have asked them on some level, they must not have pierced us to the heart. Because if we took them seriously, it would change the world as we know it. Of course it would. We are so embedded in the empire's kingdom—we are so formed by the quests we learn from being schooled in it, from breathing nonstop its empire air that we have lost our imagination for what is possible. How do you live in this world, and get a job, and have a house, and feed yourself and your family, and resist what the empire holds dear?

Jesus pushes at us to unsettle the powers-that-be and get us to participate in this endeavor—like Hagar or Esther—by hook or by crook.

It's much easier to blame the Jews or the Muslims (or the Republicans or the Democrats or the super wealthy or just someone who is not us) and—to turn the text against someone else. I'm pretty sure the good news is never that someone else is bad, though it's remarkable (or heartbreaking) how often the idea that someone else is bad, or at least worse than us, makes us feel good. Though this feeling doesn't usually lead to a human evil as extreme as the Holocaust, it certainly doesn't lead to love.

Judging is so satisfying in a sick way. Remarkably, even Martin Luther, who so often and so profoundly acknowledges that he is a sinner who needs the grace of God and who knows the depth of his need, still turns the text against a scapegoat.

I'm pretty sure that if there's good news in this text, it is that whoever exalts himself will be humbled and whoever humbles himself will be exalted. Maybe that's a beautiful promise—though it's not exactly cupcakes and ice cream.

I'm pretty sure that if there's good news in this text, it is that whoever exalts himself will be humbled and whoever humbles himself will be exalted. Maybe that's a beautiful promise— though it's not exactly cupcakes and ice cream.

Some Christians believe that the kingdom will be realized only in another life—because it isn't obvious that it happens in the here-and-now. But maybe it does. Maybe we should try wearing phylacteries or fringes so we are more aware every time they brush against our skin that God is in the mundane details of life—so that we might be more aware when we are released, even momentarily, from the need to exalt ourselves at someone else's expense.

Part Four

Mary

10 The Biblical Story
The Subversive Mother of God

Mary, ground of all being, Greetings! Greeting to you, lovely and loving Mother!

—Hildegard of Bingen

No matter how po-faced and sententious, ordered and obedient are the dreams of some ecclesiastical males, Mary seems to have a centre of gravity all of her own, one which isn't pulled in by, and submissive to, ecclesiastical constructs of what her Son would want. And God persists in gifting us with that tension, that sense of more than one centre of gravity as a relief and a freedom from the consequences of our own monistic, univocal, and frightened visions of what is acceptable.

—James Alison, *Living the Magnificat*

In the Baptist church I grew up in, we met in a multipurpose room. The folding chairs could be moved aside so the youth could play basketball. There was no art, incense, candles, or liturgy. Hearing was the one sense we indulged—choirs, hymns, soloists, and sermons—but taste, smell, touch, sight—anything that was of the body (other than the ear) was suspect.

We had potlucks, but they were about fellowship, not culinary delights. Women could teach Sunday school for girls or women's Bible studies, but they could not lead any group that included men. Not only were the senses not meant to be engaged in the house of God, but Mary also was not included.

My friend Phyllis, a counselor and professor with a flair for dressing; short, spikey, white hair; and a very long and interesting history in the church (Catholic, Celtic, nothing, Buddhist, House of Mercy), said she's noticed, "The more ritual gets cut out, the more female gets cut out."

Maybe that's part of why I can't get enough of Mary now. As Baptists, we were supposed to believe in the virgin birth, but somehow neither the *virgin* nor the *birth* was important in that formula. We were to accept both as facts of the Bible in order to uphold its literal interpretation. The *virgin* birth also conveniently emptied the gospel of sexuality. Mary was hardly mentioned—maybe once or twice at Christmas.

However much the church managed to diminish her role, there's no getting around this beautiful and stunning fact: amidst all the pages of patriarchy, the gospel of Jesus Christ begins with the Beloved Mother—a woman who gives birth to God.

But however much the Baptist church managed to diminish her role, there's no getting around this beautiful and stunning fact: amidst all the pages of patriarchy, the gospel of Jesus Christ begins with the Beloved Mother—a woman who gives birth to God.

When humans first started making things—maybe before they could talk—they drew and carved images of pregnant women (or perhaps they were just fat women, some critics say) on cave walls. Drawn and carved female images make up some of the earliest dated human artifacts. Though it's hard to know exactly how everything played out in prehistory, it's not really going too far out on a limb to say female imagery representing fertility was widespread in what we now know as Africa and Europe, India and Finland, South America and North America—all over the world—long before there were nations and empires.

Whether or not peaceful matriarchal societies existed before violent patriarchies emerged, female deities existed in central roles in almost every culture everywhere. The Great Mother Goddess may not have ruled the world (maybe *ruling* wasn't really her thing), but she was beloved in many forms all over the world.

It's no surprise that a developing monotheism might have tried to get rid of the lingering vestiges of the mother goddess, the Queen of Heaven as they tried to solidify their faith. Astonishingly, she shows up again in the first chapter of the New Testament. After all the effort of editors and priests to rid the Scripture and the temple of her presence, here she is right away, first thing: God becomes incarnate through the womb of the Mother.

In this story, Mary's womb becomes the temple out of which God emerges into the world clothed in flesh. The female presence had been suppressed for centuries, but here she is again—there are traces of Yahweh's consort that resurface in Mary—and she conceives by the Holy Spirit of God. Perhaps it was inevitable that she would show up again. No matter the efforts of the patriarchy—no matter the reasons she had been turned away, God knows we need her.

And she doesn't resurface quietly and demurely. Though the church has made a concerted effort to take the edge off

Mary, when she shows up in Luke, she almost immediately calls for the upheaval of the established order. God puts the Magnificat in her mouth—a song the Russian czars didn't like to hear sung in the Mass because its message terrified them: send the rich empty away, she says. It wasn't something they wanted the people to imagine.

In the nineteenth century the archbishop of Canterbury told his missionaries to India not to read the words of Mary because in a country with such poverty, he thought, her line about taking down the mighty could incite riots.

The Magnificat has been called "the most revolutionary document in the world." The Mother of God, by her mere existence, subverts the powers that be, and then she sings this song:

> He has brought down the powerful from
> their thrones,
> and lifted up the lowly;
> he has filled the hungry with good things,
> and sent the rich away empty.

No wonder there have been efforts to contain her by making her into a character who is meek and mild. I heard a sermon delivered by a powerful, liberal white guy who tried to empathize with Mary, describing her as a powerless teenage girl overcome unwillingly by the Spirit of God (as though she were raped and the preacher understood and was on her side). I know he meant well, but he was the one stripping her of her power: this is the woman who gives birth to God without the help of any man. None of this happens without her consent.

Mary doesn't immediately agree to this. "He whom the entire universe could not contain" will be contained in her womb (as an ancient hymn puts it). Naturally, she asks, "How can this be?" Certainly Mary couldn't understand how all this worked (who could?) but she agrees to be a part of it. Meek wouldn't be a word I'd choose for her. "Hail Mary, full of grace," the angel says—full of grace, God's most stunning attribute. She's named after Miriam, who coleads the Exodus and whose name means *rebel*.

A powerless teenage girl overcome unwillingly by the Spirit of God? I wouldn't put it that way. A subversive who somehow makes her way into the Vatican and onto the mantels of fundamentalist households in a Christmas crèche in Texas and Tennessee? Maybe that's more like it.

This story of the birth of Jesus is told in the midst of a culture where everything was structured around the passing on of the male seed—it was how you got your honor, your status, your proper place in the hierarchy. And here, in the story of Mary, the story of God becoming incarnate in the world, the male "input" is very conspicuously absent.

The church has often emphasized that because the birth was *virgin*, it was somehow spiritual, not physical. But, of course, incarnation is all about the physical. Jesus the fetus will grow a heart and lungs out of

> *Mary doesn't immediately agree to this . . . Naturally, she asks, "How can this be?" . . . Meek wouldn't be a word I'd choose for her. "Hail Mary, full of grace," the angel says—full of grace, God's most stunning attribute. She's named after Miriam, who coleads the Exodus and whose name means* rebel.

the protein Mary eats. Jesus is born like all human beings—Mary's cervix will dilate—she'll have to push. Jesus's birth very much involves the body. It didn't, however, involve the male seed. The phallus has no part in the conception of Christ, the greatest story ever told (as it is sometimes called).

Somehow, Matthew makes the story in his Gospel as much about men as possible, under the circumstances. Matthew says, "Now the birth of Jesus Christ took place in this way," and proceeds to tell us about Joseph. Joseph this. Joseph that. Joseph is a just man. Joseph resolved to divorce Mary quietly. Joseph listens to an angel who tells him not to divorce her, and somehow this makes Joseph the hero of Matthew's account of the birth of Christ. I find it a little off-putting that Matthew chooses to tell the story of a birth in this way.

The Gospel of Luke makes up for it. In Luke, the angel comes to Mary and tells her that she has been chosen to give birth to the savior. She says let it be so. She doesn't confer with her fiancé or her father. She doesn't consult with *any* man. She agrees of her own accord to conceive in her womb and bear a son.

The angel who visits Mary tells her that not only is she going to have a child but also that Elizabeth, a relative of hers, is pregnant, too. Elizabeth was old and had been called barren. To hear that she was pregnant must have seemed unbelievable. Mary immediately runs off to be with Elizabeth and together they celebrate their fertility. "Blessed is the fruit of your womb," says Elizabeth when the fetus leaps in her pregnant belly. It's all women, and wombs, and a song about overthrowing the status quo.

Western Culture Is Astoundingly Disembodied

Western culture in general has had an uncomfortable relationship with flesh—fat flesh, thin flesh, old flesh, and mortal flesh, for sure. A loathing of flesh has driven much of the history of Western thought. The yearning to escape the body has been an enormously influential desire throughout the centuries—like it would be great if we somehow could exist in the realm of pure reason, or spirit, or technology—someplace unaffected by digestion and gas. Like we would be *saved* if only we could get our minds or spirits to transcend our bodies. The body isn't something that was exactly embraced and cherished by the founders of the Western cultural and intellectual tradition.

No wonder a little of this has rubbed off on us, sometimes in very personal ways. The flesh is disconcertingly, despite sometimes heroic and sometimes desperate efforts to make it otherwise, out of our control. The hair grows uncontrollably, sometimes out of the nose—or it falls out, thins, loses its luster. The skin becomes less elastic over time. It sags and wrinkles. Of course there are Botox and plastic surgery and the gym, but you can't liposuction your way into immateriality.

We are material that is decaying rapidly (if you consider the scope of time). We are also, in our physical being, almost shockingly needy—needy of ten thousand things, like vitamins A, B, C, D, and E; sun and oxygen and water. We need to eat (many different kinds of things). The flesh may be efficient, but it's far from self-sufficient. It's contingent, and needful, and vulnerable. Those qualities and the fact that we die seem to somehow generate a preference toward a truth that is

immaterial, disembodied, spiritual as opposed to physical—
something more dignified than our organs allow.

Our preference for the immaterial has contributed to our
disregard and disrespect for the natural world. We don't respect material resources; we use them. We drill, extract, rape,
and pillage the material world. Which may explain the situation we're now in.

Christians are responsible for this as much, if not more, than
anybody, but you would think the story of the incarnate God
at the center of Christian faith could help us out here. God becomes physical, embodied, given flesh in Mary. There's no de-
nying it's an outrageous story,
with all its scandalous spec-
ificity. God comes into the
world, like all mammals, as a
cluster of cells attached to the
uterine wall nourished by the
placenta, and will be fed from
the milk of Mary's breasts. It's
God mixed up in the mole-
cules of life. Mary has a way
of keeping things grounded.

> God becomes physical,
> embodied, given flesh in
> Mary. There's no denying
> it's an outrageous story,
> with all its scandalous
> specificity. God comes
> into the world, like all
> mammals, as a cluster
> of cells attached to the
> uterine wall nourished
> by the placenta. It's God
> mixed up in the mole-
> cules of life.

I like the thought of the
ancient church Fathers (a
little prudish, patriarchal—
misogynist perhaps) having
to contend with the mother's womb. They agree eventually,
somehow—that however disturbing it might be to them on
whatever level, the body stays the scandal at the center of the
Christian faith: the incarnation of God in human flesh, forever
messing with the division between the sacred and the profane.

The Holy of Holies

After agreeing to carry God in her womb, once she's talking with her friend, Mary says, "My soul magnifies the Lord." James Alison, in his beautiful essay "Living the Magnificat" concludes that this line "means exactly what it says: God is made bigger, magnified, by Our Lady's soul. The lived-out shape of her bodily life over time is actually going to make God to be more God than before, in just the same way, I would suggest, as a really superlative operatic heroine will make Rossini be more Rossini than he was before her performance." And, of course, God is delighted to be "made more."

Alison points out that Luke uses language about Mary that refers to various stories in the Hebrew Scripture about the holy places in the Hebrew religion—the Ark of the Covenant and the tabernacle. John the fetus Baptist leaps before Mary's womb, like King David leapt before the Ark of the Covenant. The Spirit of God hovers over Mary, like the Spirit hovered over the ark and the tabernacle in the desert.

A little room in the center of the temple in Jerusalem was called the holy of holies, or the most holy place. It symbolized the place through which God made creation, says Alison— the portal through which life erupted. Once every year God's people observed an important religious holy day—the Day of Atonement.

On that day, the high priest played the role of God, who was going to come into the world. So the high priest would go into the holy of holies and dress in flowing, seamless robes. The robes were made of the same fabric as the veil that hung over the entryway of the holy of holies—the symbolic portal of creation.

At the culmination of the ceremony (everyone's standing outside singing, and excited, and someone's playing the tambourine, I imagine), the high priest walks out through the veil. And in this moment of the ceremony, it is like YHWH—the invisible, whose name you weren't even supposed to pronounce—walks out into the world and you can see God, actually visibly, materially. It was really just the high priest with a veil draped over his body, looking a little like a kid dressed up on Halloween with a sheet over his head. It was an act, a performance, a ceremonial moment, but still. In that moment it was like the divine had become visibly present in the physical world.

It was just a dress rehearsal, as Alison says.

Mary, some early writers and artists imagine, is sitting on the floor, weaving this veil for the temple that the priest is going to come through, when the angel arrives to tell her that God is going to come into the world, not through that veil, but through her womb. It's amazing how readily she agrees to this—it seems like it would be so shocking—although the text does say she was greatly troubled. I can imagine.

During her nine months of pregnancy, Mary is weaving the veil of flesh, which will make God visible in the world. Luke with his scriptural allusions suggests that all sorts of holy places came before Mary, but they were merely cultic objects used for occasional symbolic acts—things that pointed beyond themselves. Mary, a woman—not a cultic object—not something made of gold or wood, but a living human—flesh and blood—is really going to be the portal for the incarnation of God in the world. And she's not doing it in the midst of a huge and heavy sacred structure like the temple (which, like the church, was a religious institution). She is doing it as a living human being, vulnerable, alive—a mother. She is not doing this ceremoniously in an orderly way and obedient to the program set down by the ecclesiastical hierarchy.

Mary's not a little chamber made of wood in the center of the temple that the high priest enters, pretending to be God. It truly is God, so the stories go—the ever most loving, gracious, tender lover of the world who is going to emerge from her inner chamber, and no man needs to go into her first in order to come out again in different robes.

The virgin birth, however much it might have been co-opted for the ascetic purposes of the early church, isn't about calling into question the goodness of sexual generation. It's tied more to the sense of the original creation—creating something out of nothing.

Mary's going to give birth to something new. "She is living out virgin creation, new, fecund, fresh, ripe with constantly birthing possibilities, not run by men, not tied down into property or chattelage," says Alison. This creation doesn't come out of some ancient male need to propagate or control. It doesn't come from the patriarchal order of the Hebrew temple.

In the story of Mary, God puts down the mighty from their thrones: the high priest loses his place. And exalts those of low esteem: Mary and Elizabeth. And sends the rich empty away: the old holy of holies is empty now. But it's not because God hates the mighty and the rich and wants to incite the people to take up arms against the temple patriarchy. God sends the rich away because it is not through the power system that runs the world that the grace of God comes, and this graciousness is so much better than anything we could possibly construct for ourselves.

They Have No Wine

The Gospel of John doesn't have a birth narrative at all. The author starts his book by making enormous claims about Jesus—full of grace upon grace, truth, the light of every human, and then suddenly, in the second chapter, the life and light of the world through whom everything was made is at a wedding with his mom—standing around, just like everybody else, shifting their weight from one foot to the other—wondering if the food will be any good.

Jesus is about to perform the first act of his public ministry. Much is made of this—the Miracle at Cana, the First Sign. But it doesn't seem like it's really his idea. He does it because his mom tells him to. We don't see much of Mary in this Gospel, but I like this glimpse of her at the wedding.

You can find wedding imagery all over the Bible. In Isaiah, the land is married to God, who delights in her like a young man who marries a virgin. It's sort of a racy metaphor. God is married to the land and delights in it, not like an old married couple delights in each other—but like the first blush of some erotic joy. The Scripture is so weird and interesting.

Wine is all over the Bible, too. When some of the writers imagine the most passionate hope for what is to come—the great eschatological hope beyond time, at the end of ordinary reality—they imagine enormous amounts of good wine.

Amos says the mountains shall drip sweet wine, and all the hills shall flow with it. Isaiah imagines the consummation of God's kingdom as God making a feast of rich food for all the people—a feast of well-aged wines. This seems like a grace you could feel and taste—something that would satisfy you—not abstractly.

So when Jesus and his mom are at this *wedding* and she almost immediately notices "they have no *wine*," it seems like a pronouncement of doom and gloom and joyless hopelessness. And it was—not just an enormous social disgrace, but a bad sign for the couple.

In this first glimpse we have of Jesus's mother in the Gospel of John, the first words she utters are "They have no wine." It's almost like a lament. The only other time we encounter her in this book is at the foot of the cross on which her son dies. It's like she appears at the archetypal moments of human anxiety: death and the moment the wine runs out.

Some Protestant interpreters put off by "Romanist reverence of Mary" use this passage as evidence that Mary isn't really worthy of veneration—as if she was too concerned with ordinary things. Geez. You know. Hail Mary, full of grace, if you ask me. Don't we need help with ordinary things?

She doesn't come across here in the way the kitschy statues and paintings imagine her: the whole subservient, quiet handmaiden image. It's just a brief scene, obviously, but I wouldn't say from this glimpse that she really seems to worship her son (though I'm sure she loves him like crazy). She thinks he should make himself useful—he should help these people in this real moment in their real lives. I mean, if he can't really help anyone, what would be the point? Grandeur and greatness? Who. Really. Cares? What. Good. Does. That. Do? Maybe she's hoping he'll be the kind of man who is happy to help in the kitchen.

Mary is thoughtful in this scene, but Jesus doesn't come across as all that generous in this moment. Most commentaries insist that Jesus's reply to his mother is not impatient or disrespectful and maybe the words "Woman, what have you to do with me?" is code for "Thank you for giving birth to me and feeding me from your own body," but it doesn't sound like it to me. Maybe there's a better translation—but one way or the other, it seems like his agenda or purpose is more important than what's happening in the life of this family.

But prescient, grounded, intrepid Mary: she disregards her son's dismissal—like she isn't quite listening to him, like maybe she knows something. However aloof, unresponsive, and reluctant to disrupt his plans Jesus may seem—his mother really trusts him to begin his ministry here. And this first sign of palpable grace will be important. She trusts him to do something about this situation full of archetypal anxiety. There's not enough wine, or light, or warmth, or love—not enough to cover what the world needs (which is pretty vast). And even though Jesus says it's not his time, he takes direction from his mom to address the situation.

The Pieta

John is the only gospel writer who specifies that Mary the Mother of Jesus was at the foot of the cross when Jesus died. The other gospel writers all agree there were women there— the women who stayed with Jesus when the male disciples fled. John doesn't elaborate much on it, but the scene is prominent in the religious imagination.

The three verses John includes have inspired a multitude of hymns, poetry, and countless works of art—almost every painter who paints the scene puts Mary at the cross. There is no gospel writer who says Jesus is laid in the arms of his mother, but the Pieta, the image of Mary cradling the dead body of Jesus, is archetypal.

When Joseph and Mary are looking for the young Jesus in the temple, Luke says Simeon prophesied that a sword would pierce through Mary's soul. These are eloquent words for what it feels like to suffer the loss of a child—or even imagine the loss of a child, or even watch your child suffer.

The cross is the story of how Jesus participates in human suffering, and it reveals that God is present in our pain and sorrow, but I'm not sure we're always able to feel how Jesus suffered. Perhaps we can't quite relate to Jesus's suffering because he's God incarnate, he died to save the world, we're told, he's a martyr on a cross—he's not like us. But Mary's suffering is visceral for us. She watches her son die.

I can hardly get through the Stations of the Cross service we do every Good Friday without crying when we get to station four: Jesus Meets His Mother. We read the lines, "A sword of sorrow has pierced a mother's soul and has filled her heart with bitter pain." Or station thirteen, The Body of Jesus Is Placed in the Arms of His Mother: "Mary weeps and there is no one to comfort her. Share in Mary's ceaseless tears, covering her lifeless son." My son, Miles, nearly died during birth—I didn't even get to see him. They immediately flew him off in a helicopter to a children's hospital in the city. When she was twelve, Olivia had a rare and potentially deadly growth on her spine that required surgery that could have paralyzed or killed her. I have not had a dead child placed in my arms, but I have felt sick with the fear of it. I don't know how people survive the death of a child.

In all the many ways Mary would manifest to people in the ages to come, she will be seen most powerfully as someone who knows suffering. Jesus can often come across as just a little preoccupied with his mission. He certainly isn't a dispassionate stoic, but maybe his commitment to his mission makes him seem like he doesn't *feel* that much sometimes—and we need someone who understands our feeling. We need a mother (or a sister, or a friend who is not impassive, detached, or unemotional).

The cross is the story of how Jesus participates in human suffering, and it reveals that God is present in our pain and sorrow, but I'm not sure we're always able to feel how Jesus suffered. But Mary's suffering is visceral for us. She watches her son die.

In the Gospel of John, when Jesus is hanging from the cross he looks toward his mother. John writes, "When Jesus saw his mother, and the disciple whom he loved standing near, he said to his mother, 'Woman behold your son!' Then he said to the disciple, 'Behold your mother.'" Jesus doesn't say much from the cross, and what he says isn't small talk. Maybe this statement is included to show the reader that Jesus truly cared for his mother after all that whole "woman what have you to do with me" talk at the wedding. Or maybe it's an invitation to all the disciples yet to come—an invitation to anyone who follows him, "Come, behold your mother." Like he recognized our need. That would be like him—providing for us in this way: Behold your Mother.

In the Upper Room

The last time Mary appears in the gospel story is in the upper room on the day of Pentecost in Acts, ten days after Jesus ascended to heaven. Peter, James, John, Andrew, Philip,

Thomas, Bartholomew, Matthew, James, Simon, and Judas the son of James were there. Men. There were some unnamed women and Mary the mother of Jesus. I wonder if the rushing of the winds and the tongues of fire impressed her.

Mary barely surfaces in Paul's letters. He doesn't mention her by name. Galatians 4 says, "But when the time had fully come, God sent forth his Son, born of woman," or "made of a woman," or "a woman gave birth to him"—according to various translations. This is significant; obviously, God's son is made of a woman—not of God's hand pulling a rib out of Adam. Not like Zeus giving birth to Athena out of his skull. Jesus is made of a woman. But St. Paul doesn't dwell on this.

The official canon doesn't give Mary as much space as our curiosity might demand. We get to know more personal characteristics of the people in the Hebrew Scripture: David was tall, Esau was hairy, Abraham could be emotional at times, Rebecca was a trickster. The New Testament is sparse on this sort of information, so of course we wonder: Who was she?

We are left to our imaginations. In Colm Toibin's novel, *The Testament of Mary*, Mary doesn't like the disciples. She's suspicious of their project. They take care of her needs after her son dies, but they are impatient, sometimes insolent, and insensitive men bent on a mission. She doesn't believe in their mission. She feels they are responsible for her son's death. She likes the goddess Artemis, a mother goddess, who comforts her. She buys a statue of her one day when she visits her temple and whispers to her at night when the men are out of sight.

Of the Earth

In the last book of the Bible, Revelation, the author has a vision of a "woman clothed with the sun, with the moon under her feet, and on her head a crown of twelve stars." The celestial woman is attacked by dragons and gives birth to "a male child, one who is to rule all the nations with a rod of iron." She's given wings that take her to a place in the wilderness where she is nourished for a time. The serpent attacks again, "But the earth came to the help of the woman." Many interpreters see Mary in this passage in Revelation 12. It seems fitting that here, in her last appearance in the New Testament, it's the earth that comes to help her. She has done so much to keep the faith grounded.

If we somehow fail to see God incarnate in God's creation, Mary brings God into the material world again—decisively. Both the creator God and the birthed God show us a God who is in this very world. Perhaps the earth nourishes Mary in gratitude for how she nourishes it, and it cherishes her for her part in *bringing God down from heaven* (as we read in the Nicene Creed).

We need a lot of help here on this broken planet. I believe in the grace of God. But when children die, and teenagers are shot by police, and the entire Caribbean is ravaged by unprecedented hurricane damage, and the people who always get hit hard are getting hit harder, and a friend loses her twenty-two-year-old son, I don't know how the aggrieved are supposed to muster Hagar's effort. Or Esther's charms. We need their stories to give us hope and strength and ideas for resistance, but at times we are so sad, and sick, and weary that we need to be able to lie down and find rest in the arms of a mother who knows suffering, who is so well acquainted with grief. She is the woman clothed with the sun that warms us—the sun that keeps us alive even when we hardly pay attention to its presence. She brings us a God who is of the earth, not apart from it. This is the God the broken-hearted need.

11 The Shape-Shifting Queen
Goddesses, Guadalupe, and Grandmas

Living here in the City of God, I have to consider the strong possibility that God is pointedly, continually, making all things new by deliberately mixing them up.

—Sara Miles

The canonical works may not dwell on her much, but it doesn't take long in the history of Christianity before Mary becomes an object of deep devotion. The earliest known Marian prayer is from the third century: "Beneath your compassion, we take refuge, O Mother of God, do not despair our petitions in times of trouble; but rescue us from the dangers, only pure, only blessed one." Her exultation was underway. By the fifth century artistic images of Mary began to appear—eventually she would be portrayed in art and music more than any woman in the history of the world.

"It is a thought-provoking fact," says Robert Gregg in his book *Shared Stories, Rival Tellings,* "that in the several centuries prior to the eighth century outbreak of inner-Christian controversy about the use of religious pictures or icons, images of the Virgin and child greatly outnumber[ed] surviving or known images of Christ alone." An early text, possibly from

Origen, gives her the title *domina*, the feminine form of the Latin *dominus*: Lord.

The early editors of the Bible worried that the Queen of Heaven was a threat to the monotheism they promoted. Perhaps she was, but to conclude they didn't need her was editorial oversight.

Loved and imagined and reimagined by kings and queens and popes, Mary has been revered by the marginalized over and over again, by peasants and women and Brazilian jungle cults, Portuguese shepherds, Rwandan teenagers—sometimes upsetting the social order, sometimes upsetting the church hierarchy. The Mother of God does give birth to some heterodoxy, but impenetrable barriers and strict boundaries may not always be what serves the beating heart of the world.

Before the Uniformity

Before the beliefs and practices that developed around Jesus became the official religion of the empire under Constantine (around 336)—before anyone had ever insisted on or even strived for anything like Christian doctrinal uniformity, diverse beliefs appeared on the early Christian map. And the idea that there was "one right way to think about things" wasn't in the mainstream consciousness. Though the Jewish religion was well established, the Jewish tradition didn't (and still doesn't) try to convince other people to accept their belief and practice.

This meant that many ways of perceiving God and acting out a faith sat side-by-side. No overarching system governed Christian thought and belief. I'm sure it was a little chaotic, but I imagine it was lively. Lots of stories circulated about Jesus—his birth, and life, and death. And there were many stories about his mother. The stories that the community eventually deemed reliable or important were made canonical. But most of the stories of Mary remain outside the official narratives—pre-canon, post-canon, in apocryphal writing in every century: in Medjugore, Fatima, and Lourdes, in Poland, Rwanda, Egypt, and China. Authorities never successfully regulated her. People have never stopped talking about her, having visions of her, and being healed and comforted by her.

> *The stories that the community eventually deemed reliable or important were made canonical. But most of the stories of Mary remain outside the official narratives. . . . Authorities never successfully regulated her. People have never stopped talking about her, having visions of her, and being healed and comforted by her.*

There is so much Apocrypha—so much outside the canon about Mary—you could study it for a lifetime. She was conceived (immaculately) through her parents' kiss. Or she was conceived normally, but is immaculately pure. She is the ever-virgin. Or she had other children besides Jesus. Her body was taken up to heaven at the end of her earthly life, or she died and was resurrected. There are many versions of Mary.

Dancing Mary, Old Man Joseph

In the Gospel of James, written 121 years or so after the birth of Christ, Mary is said to be from a respected family. Her father is Joachim. Her mother is Anna. Her father is rich, but he and Anna are unable to have children. Anna is ridiculed for being childless. But then unexpectedly and at a ripe old age, Anna conceives (maybe through a kiss, maybe through sex—it's not entirely clear) and gives birth to Mary, a lively, precocious, unusual daughter who is given to the temple when she is three. The little girl was "delightful," this ancient apocryphal text says, and "she expressed her elevated spirit in a dance on the temple steps."

Mary lived at the temple until the onset of puberty, when she couldn't stay there anymore. Luckily, the high priest in charge got a message from God telling him that he should send her to Joseph, an old widower with young children.

In the History of Joseph the Carpenter, which expands on the Gospel of James, Mary happily cares for the youngest of Joseph's motherless children. His children are closer to Mary's age than Joseph is. In both of these versions, when the young woman in Joseph's household (whom he barely knew, really) becomes pregnant, he is alarmed. But maybe he is too old (and wise and experienced) to get all in an uproar about it. He lets it go.

Mary gives birth to Jesus. In the History of Joseph the Carpenter, Joseph recalls the birth on his deathbed, "I had never heard of a woman who conceived without a man." Joseph has a difficult death. Jesus leads the mourning and speaks the eulogy at his funeral.

Though this story of Mary doesn't reside in the biblical canon, much of Christian tradition has accepted this version of Mary's early life. When Martin Luther was a law student, he was caught in a thunderstorm on his way back to school after visiting his parents, so the story goes. Lightning struck near him and he was thrown to the ground. In this moment of fear and danger, he prayed to St. Anne, Mary's mother. "St. Anne help me! I will become a monk." He survives and keeps his promise to St. Anne. Some people see this as the moment that sets in motion the Reformation.

St. Anne is the patron saint of unmarried women, housewives, and women in labor, grandmothers, horseback riders, miners, and cabinet-makers. When I visited Germany, I saw her image all over the Lutheran churches I visited. She is often pictured holding Mary in her lap, teaching her to read.

Poor and Licentious Mary

Around 178, a version of Mary as told by Celsus starts making the rounds. We only know about his version from the objections to his version: he insisted that Jesus had invented his birth from a virgin; in fact, Mary was a poor woman who subsisted by spinning wool. She was rejected by her husband, a carpenter, because she had sex with a Roman soldier named Pantera. Jesus was the bastard son of a Roman soldier and Mary, an adulterous spinner.

Her Womb Was a Place of Great Beauty

A compelling image of Mary arises among Syriac Christians in the late first century. The Syriac Christians were clear about their identity as Jewish. They had always imagined God's presence—Shekinah they called it—as feminine. This divine feminine presence melded well with the notion of a woman, Mary, as the dwelling place of God. "The son is the cup," they wrote, "and the father is he who was milked. And the Holy Spirit is she who milked him. The womb of the virgin took it and she received conception and gave birth."

They imagined that the drama of sin and redemption was played out in a single female organ. Mary's ear: "As Eve had listened to the serpent, so Mary conceived her saving son through her ear."

Isis

Egyptian religion had a much-beloved Indigenous, formidable, mother goddess of procreation, childbirth, and fecundity: Isis. Isis had been loved in Egypt since the twenty-fourth century BCE. Christianity began to spread in the eastern Mediterranean at about the same time Isis's popularity began to peak in the same region. Soon ideas about Mary fused with ideas about Isis. The Book of the Dead describes Isis as "She who gives birth to heaven and earth, knows the orphan, knows the widow, seeks justice for the poor, and shelter for the weak."

An ancient wall painting from just south of the Nile delta (dated far earlier than the Gospels) depicts Isis holding her son on her lap, baring a breast, which she offers her son while they both look directly at the viewer in what looks very much like the iconic Madonna and child. Many statues of Isis holding Horus, her son, look like the many statues of Mary holding her son.

Isis was so loved and so loving that she found her greatest delight in the healing of humankind. She had great physical prowess and life-giving energy. She was the goddess of fertility. While I'm not considering this connection from every possible angle, this parallel does not seem threatening. I can imagine a Mary more concerned with the poor, the orphan, the widow, and the weak than with mandates to maintain a pure identity.

Theotokos

After the first Council of Ephesus in 431, held at a church in Ephesus dedicated to her a hundred years earlier, Mary is officially pronounced Theotokos, the Mother of God. Soon people began calling her the Queen of Heaven. Seriously. The title caused controversy, but was still made official. After all the efforts by the early monotheistic editors to discredit the Queen, nevertheless she persisted.

The Empire's Virgin

As Christianity and empire were being wed, the rather local, small-batch nature of Christian practices and beliefs needed to be organized, the founders believed. A coherent system was seen as a necessity. The empire needed to have a clear sense of what a Christian was, and that sense had to be dignified enough for an imperial religion. How to represent a god made flesh and his mother became an object of intense discussion. In the course of this system-making, Mary's purity—her virginity, became central to her identity.

Traditions of Christian virginity among both men and women had become popular. In the empire there was a tradition of Stoic belief and practice that thought that controlling the body—abstaining from sex—was an enormous virtue. In this period and cultural mindset, Mary became the symbol of this monastic purity.

In the words of Athanasius, "Mary was a holy virgin, having the disposition of her soul balanced. . . . She did not desire to be seen by people . . . nor did she have an eagerness to leave her house, nor was she at all acquainted with the streets; rather, she remained in her house being calm, imitating the fly in honey. And she did not permit anyone near her body unless it was covered and she controlled her anger." She read Scripture all day, never got distracted—never even looked out her window.

Not quite the lively girl dancing on the temple steps. And the complete opposite of Isis.

This version of Mary encouraged the monastic movement in its celebration of celibacy and it may have allowed some women autonomy and given them freedom not to choose marriage or motherhood. But in the text surrounding the systemizing of Mary, disturbing images abound: Ambrose, bishop of Milan and one of the most influential ecclesiastical figures of the fourth century, "delighted in describing Mary's sealed and pure body as a closed gate." Yes, there were important theological issues at stake, such as Christ's full humanity and the nature of the incarnation, but it might have ended up better for women in the long run if some of these old men had kept their minds off Mary's body.

Virginity was about separation, for Ambrose. Sexual contact blended substances best kept apart. Virgin bodies were protected from such sullying. This sort of foundational thinking—portraying sex as an act that makes people dirty—was detrimental to future prospects of healthy human sexuality (to put it mildly). It was a long time ago, I know, but I'm not sure we've gotten over it, this poisoning of Eros.

Mary #MeToo

Mary's soul magnifies the lord—it doesn't diminish him, but for all the courage and joy Mary manifests in her willingness to be the portal for God to come into the world, she does pay. She poses a problem for the patriarchy, and it's rather heartbreaking to see how, throughout the history of the church, she is man-handled, scrutinized, desexed, oversexed, and voyeuristically anatomized.

Councils of men sat around tables and discussed her reproductive apparatus. How could Jesus have come through her birth canal without breaking her seal (as they put it)? How indeed?

Luke says Mary was young, but some of the architects of the church decided she must be very young—prepubescent young. They aren't comfortable with the idea that she might have been polluted (their words) by what comes with having a biologically mature female body.

On the other hand, if you spend some time looking at Mary's image in art through the centuries, you may notice that at times her mammary glands seem rather eroticized. The Reformers noticed that too, and, horrified by what they saw as the sexualization of the Virgin in the later Middle Ages, they gathered up all the physical representations of her body they could find and burned them.

I don't think it would be crazy to say that Mary, the one woman who is actually given an indisputably prominent place in the official history of the Christian faith, has been harassed. Objectified. Received unwanted male attention. The church authorities are always trying to keep her in her place by one way or another. But, wow, do they not succeed. She does not recede.

You Can't Pin Her Down

The versions of Mary are vast, and however much the imperial version may have tried to make itself the one true version, it never worked. Mary is Our Lady of Grace, Compassion, Light, Sorrows, Mercy, Guidance, the Daughter of Zion, Seat of Wisdom, Refuge of Sinners, Mirror of Justice, Queen of Peace, Star of the Sea, Mystical Rose. She is the queen of the forest in the Santo Daime, a religion whose practice relies on drinking Ayahuasca, the psychedelic jungle brew. Some people might think she never really got a handle on the whole branding thing, because you can't pin her down. She certainly doesn't have one simple identity. But what kind of person makes herself into a brand? There is no such monolith, monotone, monoculture, or monotony with her.

Muslims as much as Catholics love and venerate Mary. She is given more attention than any other woman in the Qur'an. An entire Surah is given over to her. In the Qur'an she receives the soul or breath of God through an angel and conceives the prophet Jesus when God says, "Be!" Her pregnancy and the birth of her son are signs of God's continual creative activity in the universe. When she is in labor, God sustains her with dates that fall from a tree and a stream that springs forth in the desert. Later commentaries will compare her meeting with the angel and the miraculous stream in the desert with Hagar's encounter with Gabriel and her miraculous stream, the Zamzam well. One Sufi order names itself after Mary, Maryamiyya Sufi Tariqau, which emphasizes the divine feminine. Anse Tamara Gray believes Mary has all the qualities of an Islamic prophet, though scholars debate this.

> Mary is Our Lady of Grace, Compassion, Light, Sorrows, Mercy, Guidance, the Daughter of Zion, Seat of Wisdom, Refuge of Sinners, Mirror of Justice, Queen of Peace, Star of the Sea, Mystical Rose.

Mary Is a Bridge

Though the church's official take has most often been that Mary is more the virtuous, quiet handmaiden of God than the feminine face of God, for anyone searching and longing, whether inside or outside the official take, she effectively becomes that face. She forms a bridge to faith.

My friend Phyllis with the spiky hair and cool clothes, who grew up Catholic, remembers how every year on the first of May her church would make a crown of flowers and crown Mary queen, a practice almost certainly originating from pre-Christian goddess celebrations.

The Feast of the Assumption of Mary, the celebration of Mary's being bodily taken up into heaven at the end of her earthly life, is observed all over the world. In some places it is placed on August 15 and is clearly the Christianization of a pagan harvest festival. Herbs are blessed, and Mary is clothed in a robe covered with ears of grain. Legends say both animals and plants lose their harmful traits, poisonous snakes do not strike, and wild animals refrain from attacking humans during Our Lady's Days. Food produced during the month is said to be more wholesome and nutritious than food made at any other time of the year.

In Sicily a statue of Mary is covered in flowers and paraded through the streets. A facing procession carries a statue of Jesus. When they meet they bow three times to each other. In Italy people carry bowls of rosewater, which they sprinkle on themselves, and they throw coins out of windows. In Brazil pageants are held on decorated canoes. There's a blessing of the Alps in Austria.

Mary is a bridge: pre-Christian practice merging with church-sanctioned festivities. Is the church co-opting local Indigenous goddesses (Isis, Brigid, Tonantzin, Coatlicue, Diana), or are the goddesses just quietly crossing the bridge?

Phyllis loves the way Mary connects the old goddesses to Christianity. She says Mary tells people, "This is how you used to know me. This is how you can know me now." She says, "Mary stands in that liminal space—the space in between, opening the gate." Which is exactly why some of my Baptist friends would rather have nothing to do with her. "Having the gift of Mary," Phyllis adds, "helped me to know in a very deep way that the divine is so much bigger than we think."

Everywhere Women Are

When I speak to women who grew up Catholic they say Mary's image was everywhere—Jeanne says she was "ubiquitous in my childhood environment; in the little altar on my Italian grandmother's dresser; in prayer cards on my Irish grandmother's desk; in a statue of my mother's I still have in my bedroom; and in stories about the 'Blessed Mother.' Now that I think about it," she adds, "the image was ubiquitous only with the 'women people': Pearl and Assunta, my grandmothers; Angela, Maria Izzo, and Teresa, my cousins in Italy; and my mother."

Phyllis said there were Mary statues all over her house and her grandma's house. "She was always around—a big part of our lives." When she was old enough to start walking to her parochial school, she stopped in at the chapel every day. It was invariably full of "old nuns and grandmas, all saying the rosary—it felt like the most amazing, safest place I could ever be." She loved watching her grandma say the rosary, "her fingers moving over the beads." She went to a big Catholic church on the south side of Chicago. "There was a crucifix behind the altar. To one side was a statue of Joseph, on the other side, a statue of Mary. We always sat on the side with Mary. We talked about it as 'sitting on Mary's side.'"

Jeanne's mom, Jackie, an Irish former Catholic, expressed another sentiment I've heard from a number of women. When I asked her about her relationship with Mary, she responded

I was so devoted to her as a young woman that I named my first daughter, Mary, after her. This devotion gave me great and much-needed comfort; she filled in for my real mother who was not always "available." After I was married, she became the ideal mother image for me as my children were born, but then I became rather upset at the Church's insistence that although she was this perfect model for married women, she had to be a virgin, too. I wanted to yell, "Wait a minute!" Why must you Fathers dictate that the Ideal for Catholic women must be presented as both mother and virgin, an impossible example for a human mother to follow.... I guess I can sum it up this way: I am exceedingly grateful for all the comfort I found in her caring presence growing up—the first forty years—especially when faced with traumatic episodes. I spent hours before her statue in church, making novenas and saying the rosary. But now she's more of a bittersweet memory, one that the feminist in me rages [concerning] the Church's insistence that she be both sensual woman and virginal. Although my youth is entwined in hundreds of rosaries, I no longer belong to any established religion.

Guadalupe

I met Rebekah at House of Mercy. She attends sometimes with her mother, Kris, and her little girls, Imix and Xochitl. Her band, Lady Xok, played at our Easter service. Her father, a Catholic from El Salvador, was a parishioner in Archbishop Oscar Romero's church. After the massacre at Romero's funeral, he fled to Mexico, where he met Kris, a Norwegian from a family of pastors. Rebekah is an artist whose practice includes visual art, music, dance, and performance. Her emphasis is on Latinx/Indigenous art methods. She says her work lives in the Nepantla or in-between of Christianity and Indigeneity. She explores iconography, propaganda, decolonization, and liberation theology. She is developing a series of mixed media works that examines images of the Virgin of Guadalupe.

Guadalupe is the patron saint of Mexico. Her shrine is the most visited Catholic pilgrimage site in the world. The story around her is worth repeating. Legend has it that in 1531, an Indian named Juan Diego is passing by a hill that had been the site of an ancient temple of Tonantzin, an Aztec goddess of sustenance, Honored Grandmother. Rebekah says she's more or less "Mother Earth." In their attempt to Christianize Mexico, the Spanish colonizers had destroyed her temple. But walking past the old sight, Juan Diego is met by a vision of an Indigenous woman who claims to be Mary, the mother of God. She asks Juan to build a church for her. Juan protests that he is just a humble peasant, but he soon seeks out the Franciscan archbishop of Mexico City, who does not believe anything Juan tells him.

Juan goes back to the archbishop again, after seeing the woman another time. She asks Juan to keep pursuing the church idea. The archbishop still doesn't believe him and requests a sign.

Juan goes back to the hill to find the woman. She appears and agrees to give him a sign when he returns on the following day. But it just so happens that on the following day, Juan Diego's uncle falls sick and Juan needs to care for him, so he tries to take a different route to avoid the woman. She tracks him down and gently chides him for not asking her to help his uncle, and then in the words that have become the most famous phrase of the Guadalupe event, inscribed over the entrance to the huge basilica in her name, she says, "Am I not here, I who am your mother?"

She assures him that she will protect him and that his uncle has recovered. Then she tells him to gather flowers from the hill to bring to the church official. It is not the season for flowers and the hill is usually bare, but Juan finds a proliferation of beautiful white roses and fills his cloak with them to bring as a sign to the archbishop. When he opens his cloak before the powerful man, the flowers fall to the floor and the image of Guadalupe appears on Juan's cloak. The original cloak (so some say) still hangs in the basilica in Mexico City.

Was Guadalupe used by the Catholic Church to conquer Indigenous religion? Or did she come in and manage to subvert the male hegemony? The Franciscans were suspicious of her, but eventually she was officially recognized. Her popularity can hardly be overestimated.

The Zapatistas, the Sandinistas, and the United Farm Workers emblazoned her image on flags, and standards, and T-shirts as they carried out their struggles for justice against oppressive regimes and corporate abuse. In demonstrations against the criminalization of immigrants, the Virgin of Guadalupe can be seen on the banners of protesters. Her image is also popular with pro-life groups.

When the Santa Fe Museum of Art displayed images of Guadalupe created by Latina artist Alma Lopez depicting her as a strong, woman boxer in a rose-covered bikini, draped in a cloak with the image of the ancient Aztec goddess Coyolxauhqui, protesters threatened to shut down the museum. Some made death threats against Lopez. Many others celebrated Lopez's work as liberating and life-giving.

Guadalupe's image, a mestizo girl with her hands folded, standing on a crescent moon with a sunburst of rays emanating from her body, has become such a pop image, Rebekah says, that she wonders if it can have any sacred relevance anymore. "Seeing her image is like seeing Mickey Mouse," Rebekah says. It has been so commercialized, "it is just another pop image." As a reinterpreter of traditional folk art techniques, Rebekah makes paper cuts. She says, as a paper cutter, she's really stuck on the rays emanating from Guadalupe's image. They feel like daggers to her. Guadalupe is a weapon. She is "a reminder of terrible times, of all that has been lost." The Catholic Church is responsible for the death of Indigenous people, art, and culture. She is oppression.

The Zapatistas, the Sandinistas, and the United Farm Workers emblazoned her image on flags, and standards, and T-shirts as they carried out their struggles for justice against oppressive regimes and corporate abuse. In demonstrations against the criminalization of immigrants, the Virgin of Guadalupe can be seen on the banners of protesters.

But she's also hope. Rebekah says, "Guadalupe is a weapon but also this ephemeral bundle of roses and love." Some of Rebekah's first work as an artist was around milagros, a folk art tradition. *Milagro* means "miracle." In some areas of Latin America, people commission small paintings on tin to say thank you to a patron saint for something good that has happened to them. Some show images of gruesome things like people's fingers being sewed on and surgeries, and some are funny. Each painting includes an image of a saint. Rebekah said milagros may incorporate any saint or Jesus, but they almost always express gratitude to Guadalupe. As an artist Rebekah was interested in how the milagros work visually but also interested in how they worked in prayer.

Rebekah is not Catholic and she is skeptical of Guadalupe, but she says "there are concrete things that happen, that are sensory, that are specific to Guadalupe." She says it's like what is depicted in the milagros—when you pray you can sometimes feel a presence hovering, something she relayed to me in a story about a beloved grandmother.

When my husband's grandma Elida Gonzalez was passing, there was a moment when she was still alive but said she already felt far away and had lost her path. Everyone had been telling her it was OK for her to let go, but she wouldn't—she was always so devout to the Virgin Guadalupe. Someone in the room told her to have hope, or something like "pray to the Virgin, she'll protect you, she'll show you the way." And she responded, "What can the Virgin do for me? She can't do nothing for me." Then my Tia [aunt], who is also named Maria, and is very intuitive said she felt a dark presence in the room, what seemed like a cross on the ceiling. She was scared, so she started praying really hard to Maria to come save grandma, protect the family and the house, and kick out the bad spirit. She said she prayed, "You're not going to take her." She was so scared she closed her eyes but barely saw a shadow slip out the second-floor bedroom window. Then the room filled with the smell of roses, so strong that it was like a flower shop, as if every [image of] Guadalupe in the room (all over, in every corner) had real roses around her. There were two or three people who smelled the roses. It wasn't long after that Elida stopped speaking and passed away.

All over Latin America, Rebekah says, Mary is most important in practice and action. "But on paper she isn't the most important." She then talks about how Mary has so many different names, so many different faces. "There are Asian Marys, Indigenous Marys, Marys in all different types of clothing and different adornments. . . . Jesus isn't allowed to have the image of everyday man," she says. He's always the European-looking man with long hair and a beard. There are very few other images of Jesus. "But Mary is a saint of the everyday people." For her this really speaks to how connected people are to Mary. She says the proliferation of Marys is an example of how we can come from vastly different perspectives and still be talking about the same thing. It's beautiful from one perspective but disturbing from another. The diversity of images also shows, according to Rebekah, how Mary has been used to colonize the globe.

Aztec Dancers

Rebekah's mom, Kris, invited me to celebrate the Feast of Guadalupe at a local Episcopalian Hispanic congregation that meets in a Lutheran church.

In the sanctuary a life-size image of Guadalupe draped in lights leaned against a Christmas tree. Dozens of bouquets of white and red roses lay at her feet. I know a little Spanish, so I could make out a bit of what the priest said in his sermon. It was festive but pretty much like what you expect in a church—until the Aztec dancers came in. And then it became like no church service I've ever been to. It went from unsurprising to electrifying. Twenty or thirty dancers danced their way down the aisle in Indigenous costumes and feathers, with drums and feet flying, someone blowing through a conch shell, bare-chested men dancing vigorously. The whole place was suddenly thundering with life. The whole floor was shaking. Talk about mixing things up.

In Mexico, Kris tells me, the Aztec dancers are not allowed in the church. They dance in the square in front of the church. This gets at the mix Rebekah was talking about. The sadness of what has been lost—the hard-and-fast barriers next to something alive and hopeful.

Undermining Tyranny

Mary may look a little meek and mild and Italian at the Vatican, that all-male conclave of officials refining doctrine, but check her out as a Haitian woman smoking a Marlboro. Or as a muscular Latina in boxing gloves. She's a wealthy European aristocrat with a long elegant neck, draped in lush fabrics. She is a stout peasant with a short waist. Maybe it's because she so emphatically connects the Christian story with the physical that she is so variously represented in physical form. At St. Patrick's Guild Church Supply, you will see her in numbing conformity, but Google images of the Black Madonna—something that helped me have hope for the resistance on one of those long, hot days during the summer of 2017 when the white boys were yet again threatening the life of this planet.

It's astounding to survey how Mary has appeared over time—all across the world, shape-shifting in ways that bring life, comfort, or revolution, depending on what the people need. She doesn't demand subservience; she bends to the needs of the people.

Tyranny is the enemy of life and creativity. Mary, in so many of her guises, undermines the tyranny. She is the Black Madonna who subverts, resists, and rebels against injustice almost everywhere she shows up. In South America she is the Mother of the Excluded, Condemner of Slavery. In the Indigenous Candomble religion of Brazil, which combines Catholicism with West African and Yoruba religion—she is linked to the goddess of salt water and the goddess of sweet water. The Yoruba believe in the great mystical power of older women as protectors, healers, guardians of the social order, and just redistributors of power and wealth. According to their beliefs, the creator-God put women in charge of all the good things on earth from the beginning.

Over four hundred Black Madonnas can be found around Europe—most considered to be specially marked with sacred power. People make pilgrimages to see them. In Poland Mary is known as the Queen of the Workers, like some radical union organizer. Lech Walesa led the struggle against Polish oppression under the communist regime with an image of the Black Madonna of Częstochowa pinned to his lapel. He dedicated his Nobel Peace Prize to her. You can see it if you visit her sanctuary.

Unsanctioned Apparitions

The number and diversity of Mary's apparitions are staggering. However much they've tried, the authorities have simply failed to regulate her. She shows up in France, Ireland, Rwanda, Egypt, and Wisconsin. She appeared to three poor shepherd children in Fatima, a town in Portugal named after Muhammad's daughter, saying to them, "Don't be afraid." Fatima was Muhammad's most beloved child, the one said to resemble him most in her kindness and generosity. Fatima is revered in Islam almost as much as Mary is.

What a wondrous juxtaposition of words: Our Lady of Fatima. Our Lady (meaning Christians' Lady) of Fatima (the shining one of Islam) in one breath. At her shrine, Muslim pilgrims pray next to Christian pilgrims. Most of the pilgrims are women.

Truth isn't always something that is expressed well through doctrine. We may see it more clearly sometimes in movements toward loving relationship: Loving mercy. Shalom. Salaam. The mother who loves all of her children and wants to keep them talking to each other.

The Lady has a way with that sort of thing—creating portals, building bridges, illuminating cracks in the wall instead of fortifying the barriers.

She is not a brand. She is the mediatrix: the builder of bridges, the blurrer of lines. Though our faiths so often follow the guiding visions of the fathers, the women take us different places—places that are strange and holy, and places that mess with the lines between the sacred and the profane.

Mary will show up pretty much anywhere and everywhere—she's been seen on a grilled cheese sandwich in the

Chicago suburbs, on a pizza pan in Houston, a pretzel, a lump of firewood, a felled tree in New Jersey, a fence in Australia. She's been sighted in Cheetos, tortillas, chapattis, tea, and dental x-rays.

We might find these sorts of appearances questionable. Most are not apparitions officially approved by the Roman Catholic Church, but it would be just like her to show up for whoever needs her—grandmas, crackpots, children, the desperate, the crazies, the hungry, the starved, the uncouth. The rich and well educated are sent empty away. The poor receive their blessing.

As Jaroslov Pelikan says, "Far from being imposed on a reluctant laity by an authoritarian regime . . . belief in Marian apparitions has, as often as not, been imposed from below on the ecclesiastical authorities." Some taking down of the mighty from their thrones.

The Hope That the Mothers Bring

Mary is black. She is Mexican. Sometimes she is lily white too. She wears the masks of the Zapatistas, and you can find her tame and deferential at the Catholic bookstore—whenever, wherever, and however she is found, though, she is unfailingly true to her song. She comes for the poor. And the sick. And the wounded. For mothers who have lost their children, the tired and the oppressed.

You cannot say the same for how things have played out with the Almighty Father, who is often used by the power-ful to maintain their power. What can mobilize a contradic-tory vision to the power's totalitarian claims? The stories of women—stories that provide counter-narratives to the dominant ones—stories from the people who have so often been denied a voice. The second Vatican Council affirmed that, "Mary is a potential ecumenical bridge, a source of the future unity of all Christians." Maybe she can help lead the way into a unity even greater than "all Christians" or at least help us find a little trail through the fences that keep us divided.

We can sink into our hardened divides and stay guarded behind our boundaries, but God pretty clearly admonishes us to love our neighbors. The neighbor is someone who lives outside of the walls of the home where we feel most comfortable.

Love is notoriously hard to define, but it implies something very different than toleration—more of a deep appreciation, or a giddy sense of wonder, or a long, beautiful, and sometimes painful commitment. Whatever love is, it is not the mere assent that someone else has the right to exist. It seems a little crazy that God asks us to do this—LOVE OUR NEIGHBOR—that God thinks we might be able to, given our propensities for not loving and the human capacity for being intolerant of people who believe different things and come from different places. There are so many enemies these days—I know I feel it. But I'm guessing Jesus says love is the most important commandment because it is *crucial* for human flourishing, peace on earth, and the life of the universe (or universes).

Perhaps it is a lot for God to ask of us, but it is evidence of the overwhelming grace of God that, when you stop and give your attention to something or someone (and make yourself open to it or them), it doesn't take that long before you see some beauty. The opening might not come immediately to us or be our first impulse, but God knows we are capable of this practice. Follow the trail. Open the window. Watch where the women go.

God is not mother or father. God is not male or female. All we have are inadequate (if often beautiful) metaphors to describe God. Though God often comes across as male in the Bible and though it is full of the stories of men, the narratives of women are crucial. We need to pay attention to them and to what they open us toward.

Maybe stories of the lone charismatic-leader-man still inspire. Or maybe it's time to rethink this mythic strategy. I don't think it has been working out so well. It's had a very long run (the white, male savior myth). I think it's time to move on. Not just for the sake of women (though, of course, for them too). For the sake of the world: the generations to come—for trans, bi, Latinx, black, man, woman, and child.

It's not just women who will suffer if white men remain in their place of historic supremacy; it's anyone who is not a wealthy, healthy, white male. It is birds, trees, and plants that will suffer, along with oceans, rivers, and streams.

Though the feminine face of the divine is sometimes hard to find in the Bible, no one ever succeeded in getting rid of it entirely. Maybe because however much some groups would have liked to get rid of the traces that didn't fit their agenda, some powerful forces just couldn't be completely shoved under the rug—or maybe "powerful forces" isn't a good way to put it—maybe "truths so alive with beauty and vulnerability and the complexity of human be-ing with God" that you couldn't snuff them out.

Or maybe the God who is redeeming the world over time, in spite of shortsighted human agendas, had a hand in it. What if Hagar, Esther, and Mary were always meant to be at the table, helping us find our way? Anse Tamara, Muhammad's wives, Hend, Zamzam and Olivia, Guadalupe, Phyllis, Rebekah? Not just the men—Peter, Paul, Ambrose, Augustine, Calvin, and Luther? Hagar, Esther, and Mary bless us with more than their own stories—they give us a glimpse into a God whose love

Though the feminine face of the divine is sometimes hard to find in the Bible, no one ever succeeded in getting rid of it entirely.

is wide and all-embracing—a God who is not limited by the boundaries that human-made systems create. God is laboring to give birth to loving community, and we are all invited to participate.

Acknowledgments

I am grateful for all I have learned from reading James Alison, and from his lectures at House of Mercy. It was his use of the word "rumbustiousness" in relation to God that made me start to think about this book. His work was foundational for the sections on monotheism and Mary. I would not have been able to write the chapters on Abraham and Esther without having benefited from the genius of Avivah Gottlieb Zornberg's work. Miri Rubin's *Mother of God* contributed enormously to the chapters on Mary. I am grateful to Becky Dorf, Amina, Angel Sanchez, Meymun Mohamed, Hend Al-Mansour, Anse Tamara Gray, Wafa Qureshi, Zamzam, Amy Poppinga, Rabbi Alan Shavit-Lonstein, Phyllis Solon, Jeanne and Jacqueline DiMeglio, Rebekah Crisanta de Ybarra, Kristen Soltvedt Rinaldi, and Rev. John Marboe for talking or writing to me and allowing me to share their stories and wisdom. Thanks to Rabbi Adam Stock Spilker and Mount Zion Temple for the tremendous Esther Bible Study and Hamilton-esque Purim spiel and to Rabbi Morris Allen and the Beth Jacob congregation for welcoming me to Purim. Thanks to Rabbi Yehiel Poupko, and Rabbi Robert Cabelli, for sharing their thoughts and knowledge of Esther. Thanks to Anna Marsh for her Hebrew Bible expertise and Bishop Patricia Lull for her reading of Esther. I'm grateful to Rev. Russell Rathbun for many conversations about the Bible. Thanks to the House of Mercy community for giving me time off to write this book and for listening to me first preach many parts of this book as sermons. I'm grateful to Cyndy Rudolph for proofreading and Linda Buturian for wise early- and late-stage editorial help. Thanks to Lil Copan for her vision, encouragement, and excellent editorial guidance.

Deepest thanks to Miles Blue Larson for his thoughts and research on masculinity, and to Olivia Blue Larson for helping me think through so many things and for being a willing partner in adventures related to the book, and to Jim Larson for love and reading.

Parts of the chapters on Hagar and Esther were first published in *The Christian Century*, and an incarnation of the Hagar chapter appeared as "Spinning," in *Disquiet Time* edited by Jennifer Grant and Cathleen Falsani.

Notes

Notes to the Introduction

"Stories migrate . . . potential for change."
    Rebecca Solnit, *Hope in the Dark: Untold Histories, Wild Possibilities*, updated ed. (Chicago: Haymarket Books, 2016), 31.

"a robust commitment to hope"
    This and all the following quotations come from an episode of *On Being*.
    Krista Tippett, *On Being*, "Falling Together: An Interview with Rebecca Solnit," aired May 26, 2016.

"The intimacies of Mesopotamia died in the land of the Gospel"
    I found this quote from Jerome (Against Jovinian 1.15) and many helpful paths into the Hagar story in a book edited by Phyllis Trible and Letty M. Russell.
    Phyllis Trible and Letty M. Russell, eds., *Hagar, Sarah, and Their Children* (Louisville: Westminster John Knox, 2006), 133.

Princeton University professor Keeanga-Yamahtta Taylor, said
    You can listen to her entire speech at https://www.youtube.com/watch?v=6ljTRRVuUjM

"Truth is the sort of thing . . . could alone."
    When I looked back to find this quote that inspired me, I realized

Abby is paraphrasing another author who was paraphrasing Bakhtin, the Russian philosopher, but however I mangled it, I couldn't stop thinking about it. I first read the quote in a paper Abby wrote, "Reader, Author, Character: A Confusion of Roles in the Borgesian Book of Job" by Abigail Pelham. Her essay was later published in the following book:

Borges and the Bible, ed. Richard Walsh and Jay Twomey (University of Sheffield: Sheffield Phoenix Press, 2015).

"If there were only . . . pleasure of finding."

Robert C. Gregg, *Shared Stories, Rival Tellings: Early Encounters of Jews, Christians, and Muslims* (New York: Oxford University Press, 2015), xviii.

Notes to Chapter One

"Only when stability is lost . . . the means by which standing is achieved."

Avivah Gottlieb Zornberg, *The Murmuring Deep: Reflections on the Biblical Unconscious* (New York: Shocken Books, 2009), 162.

"God made me wander."

Genesis 20:13, New English Translation

"Go from your . . . house."

Genesis 12:1, RSV

"Look at that foolish, crazy old . . . madman."

My reading of Abraham's story relies heavily on Zornberg's book—it is through her that I learned about midrash. I rely on her interpretations throughout the book. The above isn't an exact quote from the midrash but the gist of it.

Avivah Gottlieb Zornberg, *The Beginning of Desire: Reflections on Genesis* (New York: Doubleday, 1995), 76.

Zornberg . . . suggests it's his willingness . . . that qualifies him.

Zornberg, *The Beginning of Desire*, 80–89.

in the "waste space between clarities . . . radical astonishment abides."
Zornberg, *The Beginning of Desire*, 90–91.

"I will make you exceedingly fruitful."
Genesis 17:6, RSV

"I am just an alien and a sojourner among you."
Genesis 23:4, RSV

"Abraham died old and contented—in a ripe age."
Genesis 25:8, NAS

Notes to Chapter Two

"This I think . . . loved."
It was reading this essay by James Alison that started me thinking about this book. I loved this idea of the "rumbustiousness of God whose monotheism is decidedly unhygienic." (*Rumbustiousness* is a British word for *rambunctiousness*.) I highly recommend reading "Living the Magnificat," which you can find online as well as in the following book of essays. Alison's influence on how I've come to think of many things is enormous.
James Alison, *Broken Hearts and New Creations: Intimations of a Great Reversal* (London: Continuum, 2010), 32.

"monotheism without contemplation is dangerous"
James Alison, *Undergoing God: Dispatches from the Scene of a Break-in* (New York: Continuum, 2006), 17.

Jeremiah's objections to her
Jeremiah 7:18; 44:17–25

a mother bear
Hosea 13:8

a mother eagle
Deuteronomy 32:11–12

a woman who gives birth
  Deuteronomy 32:18, Isaiah 42:14

a nursing mother
  Isaiah 49:15, Isaiah 66:13, Hosea 11:3–4

a midwife
  Psalm 22:9–10

"the skull, and the feet, . . . hands"
  2 Kings 9:35, RSV

It might be helpful, Alison suggests, to think less of the number
  Alison, *Undergoing God*, 18.

"essentially relational, ecstatic, fecund, alive as passionate love"
  Catherine LaCugna, *God for Us: The Trinity and the Christian Life*
(San Francisco: Harper and Row, 1991), 1.

"self-indulgent guess work . . . know or prove"
  Karen Armstrong, *A History of God: The 4,000-Year Quest of Judaism, Christianity and Islam* (New York: Knopf, 1993), 143.

"eateth not the bread of idleness"
  Proverbs 31:27, KJV

"riseth also while it is yet night, and giveth meat to her household"
  Proverbs 31:13, KJV

"excreted neither feces . . . tears from her eyes"
  Carolyn Walker Bynum, *Holy Feast and Holy Fast: The Religious Significance of Food to Medieval Women* (Berkeley: University of California Press, 1987), 211.

Saint Ida of Louvain . . . didn't want anything to pass her lips that tasted pleasant
  Bynum, *Holy Feast and Holy Fast*, 119.

Notes to Chapter Three

"Your task is not to seek for love . . . within yourself that you have built against it."

I found this quote in a book of essays by a diverse array of Muslim women. Reading this book did much to broaden my view.

Maria M. Ebrahimji and Zahra T. Suratwala, eds., *I Speak for Myself: American Women on Being Muslim* (Ashland, OR: White Cloud Press, 2011), 162.

"Any good poem . . . spins against the way it drives."

As soon as I heard this quote I thought of the Hebrew bible. It is such an apt description of its goodness. The quote is from an interview with David Milch, the creator of *Deadwood*, the HBO series. I saw it on one of the extras on the DVD version when I was running on my treadmill. You can see it here:

"The Education of Bullock vs Swearengen," https://www.youtube .com/watch?v=_HwS_m2Kh9s.

"The Other Border Wall Project"

The only requirement for passing through the pipe organ wall is that one must spend at least two minutes playing the piano. The drinkable wall and the hammock wall are not meant to exclude but to restore weary travelers.

See https://www.otherborderwallproject.com.

"such as there has never been, nor ever shall be again."
Exodus 11:6 RSV

Paul's argument about Hagar in Galatians
Galatians 4:22–31

"wild and intractable temper"

I found the discussion of Luther and Calvin in that instructive book I previously mentioned, edited by Letty Russell and Phyllis Trible.

Phyllis Trible and Letty M. Russell, eds., *Hagar, Sarah, and Their Children* (Louisville: Westminster John Knox Press, 2006), 19.

"For more . . . black folks."
Delores S. Williams, *Sisters in the Wilderness: The Challenge of Womanist God-Talk* (New York: Orbis Books, 1993), 2.

"Hagar becomes the first . . . power structures"
Williams, *Sisters in the Wilderness*, 19.

The God Who Sees
While working on this book, I published an article in *The Christian Century* about Hagar. My essay about her also appeared in a book of unconventional reflections on scriptural passages. Some of the wording in this chapter first appeared in those places.
Debbie Blue, "The Other Woman," *The Christian Century,* November 24, 2014.
Jennifer Grant and Cathleen Falsani, eds., *Disquiet Time: Rants and Reflections on the Good Book by the Skeptical, the Faithful, and a Few Scoundrels* (New York: Jericho Books, 2014), 15–23.

Sarah deals "harshly with her"
Genesis 16:6, RSV

"you must not mistreat or oppress"
Exodus 22:21, New Living Translation

"Behold, you are . . . Ishmael."
Genesis 16:11, RSV

"I will so greatly . . . multitude."
Genesis 16:10, RSV

"a wild ass of a man"
Genesis 16:12, RSV

"The son of the slave . . . my son."
Genesis 21:10, RSV

"Lift up the lad . . . nation."
Genesis 21:18, RSV

"Take your son . . . burnt offering."
Genesis 22:2, RSV

The story starts receiving more attention at the end of the first millennium BCE
Bruce Feiler, *Abraham: A Journey to the Heart of Three Faiths* (New York: Harper Perennial, 2005), 108.

"this willingness to make the 'ultimate sacrifice' . . . divine centered world."
Feiler, *Abraham,* 108.

"suppressed his compassion in order to perform thy will with a perfect heart."
These lines are included in a Jewish prayer recited during the services of Rosh Hashanah.
Quoted in Athalya Brenner, ed., *Genesis: A Feminist Companion to the Bible, Second Series* (Sheffield: Sheffield Academic Press, 1998), 135

Abraham marries Keturah
Genesis 25:1

Notes to Chapter Four

"Suppose we admitted for the sake of argument that motherhood was powerful."
I found this quote by Laurel Thatcher Ulrich in a chapter about images of God as a laboring woman in Lauren Winner's wonderful and nourishing book.

Lauren Winner, *Wearing God: Clothing, Laughter, Fire, and Other Overlooked Ways of Meeting God* (New York: Harper One, 2015), 149.

"Transcend literally means . . . to cross over, to bridge, or to make connections. . . . We have 'stuck God' with a notion of transcendence that is a projection of those who are used to being in charge."
Karen Bloomquist, "Let God Be God: The Theological Necessity of Depatriarchalizing God," in *Our Naming of God*, ed. Carl Braaten (Minneapolis: Fortress Press, 1989), 55.

"if you're rubbing shoulders with a lot of Muslims"
John Enger, "Anti-Islam Speakers Urge Rural MN Crowds to Prepare for Muslim Attack," Minnesota Public Radio, October 25, 2016.

"Saying Islam meaningfully . . . objects associated with Islam."
I didn't actually read Shahab Ahmed's work, though I would like to. I found this information in a book review in *The Nation* magazine.
Elias Muhanna, "Contradiction and Diversity: A Review of *What Is Islam?* by Shahab Ahmed," *The Nation*, January 11, 2016.

Notes to Chapter Five

"Islam is, at its core, a religion of dissent. It is not premised on an endless list of do's and don't's, but is instead multifarious and openly accepting of multiplicity."
Asma T. Uddin, "Conquering Veils: Gender and Islams," in *I Speak for Myself: American Women on Being Muslim*, ed. Maria M. Ebrahimji and Zahra T. Suratwala (Ashland, OR: White Cloud Press, 2011), 40–41.

"Islam is the first feminism."
From my conversation with Anse Tamara Gray.

"dedicated to promoting positive . . . female voice in scholarship."
See rabata.org

Hagar is not named specifically in the Qur'an, but she is present as the mother of Ishmael.

Surah 14:35–41; 2:158

Notes to Chapter Six

"Next time someone sees her in hijab*, she concludes, 'Don't look at me sympathetically. I am not under duress or a male-worshipping female captive from those barbarous Arabic deserts. I've been liberated.'"*

These are the words of Sultana Yusufali, a seventeen-year-old high school student, quoted in:

Katherine Bullock, *Rethinking Muslim Women and the Veil: Challenging Historical and Modern Stereotypes* (London: The International Institute of Islamic Thought, 2002), 185.

"Generous listening is powered by curiosity, a virtue we can invite and nurture in ourselves to render it instinctive. It involves a kind of vulnerability—a willingness to be surprised, to let go of assumptions and take in ambiguity."

Krista Tippett, *Becoming Wise: An Inquiry into the Mystery and Art of Living* (New York: Penguin, 2016), 29.

Many young Muslim women choose to wear hijab as a rebellion against consumer capitalism, with its objectification and commodification of the female body. . . . They see hijab "as an empowering tool of resistance."

Bullock, *Rethinking Muslim Women and the Veil,* 216.

"Paradise lies at the feet of the mother."
"Who should be my most honored companion?"

I first heard these stories from Imam Samir Saikali at a presentation he made at St. Thomas Becket Church, Eagan, MN. But they are widely known and repeated. In lieu of finding them in the original hadith, you can find them here:

Deane Morgan, *Essential Islam: A Comprehensive Guide to Belief and Practice* (Santa Barbara: ABC-CLIO, 2010), 192.

Notes to Chapter Seven

"For I conclude that the enemy . . our own revolution."
This quote is ubiquitous on the Internet, and you can find it a thousand places. Here's one:
Quoted in Ellen T. Crenshaw, "We Are Entitled to Wear Cowboy Boots to Our Own Revolution," thenib.com, March 8, 2015.

John Calvin and Martin Luther on Esther
Karen H. Jobes, *The NIV Application Commentary: Esther* (Grand Rapids: Zondervan, 2011), 21.

The rabbis . . . comment on the book of Esther more than any other book in the Bible besides Genesis.
I learned this surprising piece of information, along with other valuable thoughts on Esther, while listening to an interview on Interfaith Voices,
Maureen Fielder with Yoram Hazony, "Queen Esther's Newfound Popularity," *Interfaithradio.org*, March 22, 2016.

Esther steps out of the pages of Scripture and argues for herself
Hayim Nahman Bialik, Yehoshua and Hana Ravnitzky, eds., *The Book of Legends Sefer Ha-aggadah: Legends from the Talmud and Midrash*, trans. William G. Braude (New York: Schocken Books, 1992), 447.

listed in the Talmud as the last of the seven prophetesses
Avivah Zornberg, *The Murmuring Deep: Reflections on the Biblical Unconscious* (New York: Schocken Books, 2009), 121.

Maimonides . . . will be celebrated into infinity.
Zornberg, *Murmuring Deep*, 115–16.

The rock sinks when it believes it can walk on water
I learned this humorous reading of Peter the Sinking Rock from John Linton, a professor of biblical studies at the Oregon Extension in Ashland, Oregon. I learned much more than this from him—without

John as a teacher, I would not have been very interested in studying the Bible. I wish he wrote books so I could direct you to them.

"The midrash invites us to read the text with . . . available to us."
Avivah Gottlieb Zornberg, *The Beginning of Desire: Reflections on Genesis* (New York: Doubleday, 1995), xv.

"The riches of his royal glory and the splendor and pomp of his majesty."
Esther 1:4, RSV

"Everybody who's rich, powerful . . . that was Xerxes."
"When no women are present . . . Amen?"
Mark Driscoll, "Esther 1:1–9: Jesus Is a Better King," *Mars Hill Church Archive*, September 16, 2012.
(http://marshill.se/marshill/media/esther/jesus-is-a-better-king)

"quite in order to assume . . . Joseph's story."
Quoted in Athalya Brenner, ed., *Ruth and Esther: A Feminist Companion to the Bible, Second Series* (Sheffield: Sheffield Academic Press, 1999), 242.

"protest against the breaking and silencing of female power."
Quoted in Brenner, *Ruth and Esther*, 242.

"The story links fight against sexist power . . . according to Butting."
Cited in Brenner, *Ruth and Esther*, 245.

On Esther's age
Gen Rabbah 39:13, Abba Gurion, para 20
Tamara Meir, "Esther: Midrash and Aggadah," *Jewish Women's Archive*, jwa.org.

"You know all things . . . glory of God."
Esther with Additions 13:12–14, NRSV, HarperCollins Study Bible with Apocryphal/Deuterocannonical Books, Student Edition.

"to destroy, to slay . . . twelfth month"
Esther 3:13, RSV

"to keep silence at such a time as this."
Esther 4:14, RSV

"Will he even assault the queen . . . my own house?"
Esther 7:8, RSV

"Esther is a kind of Jesus . . . salvation of the Jews."
Sam Wells, "For Such a Time as This," *Faith and Leadership Online Journal*, February 1, 2009.

"My God, my God why hast thou forsaken me?"
Psalm 22:1, RSV

womanish (*as Alice Walker defined it*
Alice Walker, *In Search of Our Mothers' Gardens: Womanist Prose*, reprint ed. (Boston: Mariner Books, 2003), xi.

"like the deer pants for water."
Psalm 42:1, *The Living Bible*

The pope even quoted Nietzsche
I learned about Pope Benedict XVI's first papal encyclical from an essay in an online edition of a periodical.
D. C. Schindler, "The Redemption of Eros: Philosophical Reflections on Benedict XVI's First Encyclical," *Communio International Catholic Review*, Fall 2006.

"Beauty will save the world."
Fyodor Dostoevsky, *The Idiot*, Vintage Classics reprint ed. (New York: Random House, 2005), 526.

Notes to Chapter Eight

"There is a thin line that separates laughter and pain, comedy and tragedy, humor and hurt."
 Erma Bombeck, *If Life Is a Bowl of Cherries, What Am I Doing in the Pits?* (New York: McGraw Hill, 1998), page one of chapter 14.

"These days should be remembered . . . among the Jews."
 Esther 6:28, RSV

For the NPR interview on Purim:
 Deena Prichep, "Jewish Synagogues Celebrate Purim Plays," *NPR Weekend Edition*, March 11, 2017.

"Tragedy proclaims the grandeur of humankind. Comedy tells us the grandeur is a sham."
 Abigail Pelham, "Job as Comedy, Revisited," *Journal for the Study of the Old Testament* 35:1 (2010), 110.

Notes to Chapter Nine

"Teach your tongue to say, 'I don't know,' lest you be exposed as a liar."
 The Talmud, B. Berachoth 4a

"I was born when all I once
feared—I could
love."
 Rab'ia al Basr was a Sufi mystic and poet from the eighth century. You can find these words in the poem "Die Before You Die" in the following book:
 Daniel Ladinsky, *Love Poems from God: Twelve Sacred Voices from the East and West* (London: Penguin, 2002), 7.

"He was there for six days . . . so that they would devour Daniel."
 Bel and the Dragon (Chapter 14 of the Greek Version of Daniel), vv. 31–32, NRSV

At the ritual Passover Seder meal . . . questions propel the narratives of faith to keep having meaning for the generations.

You can find this idea expressed throughout Zornberg's work. There is a great discussion in one of her interviews with Krista Tippett.

Krista Tippett, *On Being*, "The Transformation of Pharoah, Moses, and God: An Interview with Avivah Zornberg," aired April 10, 2014.

"a base, whoring people. . . . We are at fault in not slaying them."

All quotes from Martin Luther, "On the Jews and Their Lies," *Luther's Works*, trans. Martin H. Bertram (Philadelphia: Fortress, 1971).

"seeking God in their midst."

Avivah Zornberg, *The Particulars of Rapture: Reflections on Exodus* (New York: Doubleday, 2001), 2.

Notes to Chapter Ten

"Mary, ground of all being, Greetings! Greeting to you, lovely and loving Mother!"

This is a prayer from Hildegard of Bingen, the German Benedictine abbess of the twelfth century. She is a wonderful example of how, when women have been able to play a part in religious formation, they include the Mother. You can find this blessing, along with others, in the following book:

Matthew Fox, *Original Blessing: A Primer in Creation Spirituality, Presented in Four Paths, Twenty-Six Themes, and Two Questions* (New York: Torcher/Putnam edition, 2000), 221.

"No matter how po-faced . . . of what is acceptable."

James Alison, *Broken Hearts and New Creations: Intimations of a Great Reversal* (London: Continuum, 2010), 32.

Russian czars and archbishop of Canterbury's fear of the Magnificat

I have heard these statements in a number of sermons. One place where I found them online: http://thejournalofaspiritualwonderer .blogspot.com/2015/11/the-birth-of-revolution.html.

Padre James, "The Birth of a Revolution," *The Journal of a Spiritual Wanderer,* November 3, 2015.

He has brought down the powerful . . . and sent the rich away empty.
Luke 2:52–53, RSV

"He whom the entire universe could not contain was contained within your womb, O Theotokos."
See https://aleteia.org/2017/10/11/how-theotokos-became-the-perfect-title-of-the-virgin-mary/

"Now the birth of Jesus Christ took place in this way."
Matthew 1:18, RSV

"Blessed is the fruit of your womb."
Luke 1:42, RSV

"means exactly what it says . . . operatic heroine."
Alison, *Broken Hearts and New Creations,* 19.

"She is living out . . . into property or chattelage."
Alison, *Broken Hearts and New Creations,* 27.

The land is married to God, who delights in her like a young man who marries a virgin.
Isaiah 62

They imagine enormous amounts of good wine.
Amos 9:13–15

"They have no wine."
John 2:3; RSV

"Romanist reverence of Mary"
Edward Jewitt Robinson, *The Mother of Jesus, Not the Papal Mary* (Wesleyan Conference Office, 1875: digitalized August 29, 2006), 153–59.

"When Jesus saw his mother. . . . 'Behold your mother.'"
    John 19:26, RSV

In Colm Toibin's novel
    One thing I liked in this fictional story of Mary was that she seemed a little tired of the all-male conclave, and she longed for the feminine face of God just as so many women have.
    Colm Toibin, *The Testament of Mary* (New York: Scribner, 2012).

"a woman clothed with the sun, with the moon under her feet . . . crown of twelve stars."
    Revelation 12:1, RSV

"A male child, one who is to rule . . . rod of iron."
    Revelation 12:5, RSV

"But the earth came to the help of the woman."
    Revelation 12:16, RSV

Notes to Chapter Eleven

"Living here in the City of God, I have to consider the strong possibility that God is pointedly, continually, making all things new by deliberately mixing them up."
    Sara Miles, *City of God: Faith in the Streets* (New York: Jericho Books, 2014), 149.

"Beneath your compassion, we take refuge, O Mother of God . . . only blessed one."
    Daniel Esparza, "Let Us Pray: The Earliest Known Marian Prayer," *Aleteia.org*, July 8, 2016.

"It is a thought-provoking . . . surviving or known images of Christ alone."
    Robert C. Gregg, *Shared Stories, Rival Tellings: Early Encounters*

of Jews, Christians, and Muslims (New York: Oxford University Press, 2015), 492.

"delightful . . . dance on the temple steps."
The early history of Mary that I trace in chapter eleven is heavily dependent on the wonderful treatment I found in this book.
Miri Rubin, *Mother of God: A History of the Virgin Mary* (New Haven: Yale University Press, 2009), 10.

Mary happily cares for the youngest of Joseph's motherless children.
Rubin, *Mother of God,* 12.

"I had never heard of a woman who conceived without a man."
Rubin, *Mother of God,* 12.

"The son is the cup. . . . conception and gave birth."
Rubin, *Mother of God,* 35.

"As Eve had listened . . . through her ear."
Rubin, *Mother of God,* 37.

"She who gives birth to heaven . . . and shelter for the weak."
Hazel Butler, "The Cult of Isis and Early Christianity," *Hohonu: A Journal of Academic Writing,* 7 (2005).

An ancient wall painting . . . directly at the viewer
Rubin, *Mother of God,* 41.

"Mary was a holy virgin, having the disposition . . . she controlled her anger."
Rubin, *Mother of God,* 23–24.

She read Scripture . . . looked out her window.
Rubin, *Mother of God,* 24.

"delighted in describing Mary's sealed and pure body as a closed gate."
Rubin, *Mother of God,* 27.

In the Qur'an she receives the soul or breath of God through an angel.
    Gregg, *Shared Stories, Rival Tellings,* 560.

Was Guadalupe used by the Catholic Church to conquer Indigenous religion? Or did she come in and somehow manage to subvert the male hegemony?
    Sara Miles asks a similar question in her book *City of God,* which I have thought of ever since I first read the book, and which influenced my chapter on Mary. I love how Miles writes about Guadalupe and the mestizaje—the combining of culture and religion that happens in Mary. I have often turned back to her discussion of Guadalupe because it gives me such hope. I highly recommend *City of God* and all that Miles has ever written.
    Sara Miles, *City of God: Faith in the Streets* (New York: Jericho Books, 2014), 154.

Latina artist Alma Lopez. . . . threats against Lopez.
    Alicia Gasper de Alba and Alma Lopez, eds., *Our Lady of Controversy: Alma Lopez's Irreverent Apparition* (Austin: University of Texas Press, 2011), 3.

Haitian woman smoking a Marlboro
    Sonti Ramirez, "The Many Faces of the Black Madonna of Częstochowa," *Krakow Post,* November 2, 2013.

Muscular Latina woman in boxing gloves
    Lopez, *Our Lady of Controversy,* 287.
    The image is called *Our Lady of Controversy II.* It is in an acrylic painting by Alma Lopez, 2008.

In the Indigenous Candomble religion
    Malgorzata Oleskiewicz-Peralba, *The Black Madonna in Latin America and Europe: Tradition and Transformation* (Albuquerque: University of New Mexico Press, 2007), 83.

The Yoruba believe in the great mystical power of older women
    Oleskiewicz-Peralba, *The Black Madonna,* 97.

"Far from being imposed on a reluctant laity . . . below on ecclesiastical authorities."

Jaroslav Pelikan, *Mary through the Centuries: Her Place in the History of Culture* (New Haven: Yale University Press, 1996), 186.

"Mary is a potential ecumenical bridge, a source of the future unity of all Christians."

Jason Byassee, "What about Mary? Protestants and Marian Devotion," *The Christian Century*, December 14, 2004.

Reader's Guide and Discussion Group Questions for
Consider the Women: A Provocative Guide to
Three Matriarchs of the Bible

Introduction

> . . . these stories seem to have an endless capacity to reveal
> glimpses of God, what it is to be human, things we might
> rather keep hidden, what is under the surface of everyday
> life. I am grateful for these stories that persist in baffling and
> nourishing me. (See p. 2.)

1. Though religious readers worry that fewer and fewer people are biblically literate, biblical stories continue to influence
culture in profound and lasting ways. Where do you see this
happening (for better or worse)? Do you find that the Bible
continues to have a capacity to reveal truths in your life? In
the life of the world?

> One of the beautiful things about having a canon is that
> you can look back and see an endless matrix of interpreta-
> tion unrolling over hundreds, even thousands, of years. The
> stories are told and retold, stretched, and excavated. They
> are read differently in every age—forever generating new
> meanings and new life for people in the times and places
> where they live. (See p. 4.)

2. Stories change according to who tells them and how they are told. For much of history the official storytellers in the monotheistic faiths have been men. Have you experienced a story differently depending on who was telling it? What was the story and how did it affect you?

3. We usually hear Bible stories told from the perspective of the faith tradition with which we most closely identify. How do the stories look different when told by someone looking with a different lens? From a different faith tradition?

> If you value only the strong, then you don't value the weak. I know many people, men and women, who fear the revelation of their vulnerability more than almost anything. That's a narrative that needs to be transformed. (See p. 7.)

4. We often feel we need to project strength in order to protect ourselves. But often this sort of armor keeps us from intimacy and honesty, both with ourselves and with others. It doesn't always strengthen community. Do you fear the revelation of your vulnerability? If so, why do you think it's scary? What might change in our families, communities, and nation if we were honest about vulnerability? Could we breach some divides? How could being vulnerable make communities stronger?

> These are some wild and provocative women. And they keep on living off the page over the centuries, impacting and enlivening human culture from Mecca to Mexico and everywhere in between. (See p. 8.)

5. Women have not often been in the forefront of the Abra-hamic faiths—they are not often considered to be the leading figures. What biblical women have you encountered who have impacted you, both on and off the page?

Part One: Abrahamic Faith

Chapter One
Go from Your Father's House:
Moving to New and Unknown Places

Abraham was old, and he didn't shave, and he had bad teeth, almost certainly. His wife was old and barren, and she may once have been pretty, but probably not TV-preacher's-wife pretty. His children wouldn't be described as "happy." Isaac and Abraham never speak, in the biblical account, after the scene on Mount Moriah. If God's bless-ing begins with Abraham's story, it turns out to be a very odd, complicated, and shot-through-with-a-thousand-fragments-of-everything sort of a blessing. *Blessing* is even a weird word to use for what Abraham gets when he starts getting faith. (See p. 15.)

1. In this chapter the author offers a reading of the Abraham saga that suggests faith might be less about adhering to a par-ticular system and more about letting go of what you think you know in order to glimpse what you don't know yet. How does or doesn't this ring true to your experience of faith? If you are a part of a religious community, does it foster this view of faith? In what ways does it do so? In what ways does it not?

2. In your experience, how does faith involve a complicated range of "blessings"?

3. Adherents of the Abrahamic faiths have often committed violence in the name of God. Yet they have also contributed to peaceful resolutions and the common good. What sorts of attitudes or ways of being contribute to peace? What attitudes and ways of being contribute to violence?

Chapter Two
Rambunctious Monotheism:
The Feminine Face of God

> The Bible has a lively abundance—an unruly surplus of metaphors—when it tries to speak of God. God is unique, hard to describe, impossible to contain. But in order to speak of God, in order to communicate, we point widely and wildly. (See p. 23.)

1. The author tries to make the case that worshipping one God—believing in one God—does not necessarily mean that God is monolithic. There is room for the feminine face of God as well as other metaphors, and we might do well to amplify the feminine ones. Do you agree? How might this shift your image of God? There are many metaphors for God in the Bible. Name as many as you can. Do you experience God as a lion? A lamb? Dew? What metaphors are most meaningful to you?

> The women in the Bible generally don't conform to the image of the virtuous woman I learned in Sunday school.

They don't look like good evangelicals. Or like the medieval Christian saints—women who, according to the men who wrote about them, were not interested in food, sex, or pleasure of any kind. (See pp. 25–26.)

2. The Christian tradition has historically held rather confining roles for women, with men usually defining these roles. Yet despite these attempts, the women were not confined. Think about the stories of women in the Bible. Do they seem to fit their narrow "saint-like" definition? How would you define a virtuous woman? Is it different from the definition you learned growing up, and how so?

. . . women in the Bible are more subversive than subservient. Rather than fit seamlessly into the patriarchal narratives, they disrupt them.

Hagar is blessed in the same way Abraham is: giving birth to a whole people—a whole other faith, as it turns out. Esther saves her people not through being pure or virginal—quite the opposite. Mary the mother of Jesus is, well, the mother of God. To say these stories are edgy is to minimize them. They undermine the dominant patriarchal narrative in significant ways. (See p. 27.)

3. When you remove the lens of patriarchy, you can start to see women characters in a new light. This book focuses on Hagar, Esther, and Mary, but what other biblical women don't conform? What other women subvert the dominant paradigm?

Part Two: Hagar

Chapter Three
The Biblical Story:
A Matriarch on Par with a Patriarch

> We need the Good News. We need a story about a God
> acting against overwhelming forces of injustice, a God who
> doesn't side with power. The story of Hagar is one of those
> stories—one where God makes a way out of no way. (See
> p. 32.)

1. Many stories in the Bible deal with the question of how the
people of God interact with the powers that be. What other
stories can you think of where God makes a way out of no
way—where God sides with the outsider or the powerless?

> People often read the stories as if they were meant to create
> a sense of "us" and "them," but that way of reading misses
> the pulsing, merciful heart of Scripture. The word of God is
> a revelation meant to bind us to each other and God—not
> to enforce enemy lines. (See p. 34.)

2. Though the Bible has often been used to defend an "us"
against "them" mentality, do you think it's possible to read it
in a different way? How might the world change if we gave up
scapegoating one another?

> The grand narrative in Genesis is about Israel. It's about
> Abraham's heirs through Isaac—and God's blessing of the

Jewish people. Hagar's story thrusts out in an entirely different direction, with Abraham's other son and the other woman.

Hagar's name means *other, outsider, stranger*. Who let her in? (See p. 36.)

3. What do these sorts of disruptions in the narrative suggest to you? What happens when a grand narrative ignores "the other" or makes "the other" the enemy?

When the water is gone, Hagar places her dying child under a bush and sits down and pleads, "Please don't make me watch my boy die." Again, a first. This is the most emotion we've seen displayed in the Bible so far. Hagar is the first person in the Bible to weep. Hagar reaches out emotionally to the God who sees and God sees her. God tells her not to be afraid. "Lift up the lad and hold him fast with your hand; for I will make of him a great nation."

In the narrative of Genesis you don't see God acting quite so mercifully and tenderly in response to humans until you see God with Hagar. (See p. 40.)

4. Depending on the tradition or family you come from, emotion may or may not be viewed as an acceptable way to reach out to God. Does God seem like a tender character to you? How do you believe God responds to the vulnerable? What about the earthly powers—how do they respond to the vulnerable?

Maybe we've been focusing on the wrong story. Look at the mother, because her story is here, too—the matriarch on par with the patriarch. (See p. 43.)

5. The author compares the story of Abraham and Isaac to the story of Hagar and Ishmael. As you put the stories side by side, what do you see? The willingness to sacrifice what you love to God has often been viewed by religions as virtuous. Is there a way to see it differently? When you glimpse what faith looks like through the matriarchal lens, does it look the same anymore? In what ways?

Chapter Four
The Mother of Islam:
Looking for Hagar in the Qur'an, a Tattoo Parlor, and an Art Gallery

The Ka'aba, located in Mecca, is the holiest shrine in Islam. According to Islamic tradition, it was first built by Adam and then rebuilt later by Abraham and Ishmael when Abraham came to visit his son. When Abraham leaves Hagar and Ishmael in the wilderness, he leaves them at the Ka'aba site, "The House of God." (See p. 46.)

1. If we see the Bible's primary mode of revelation to be story, what does it mean when various groups take up these stories and continue them or tell them in a new way? Does canon somehow forbid us to imagine beyond its strict limits? Or might we be free to do so?

I worried a little that if I followed Hagar into her Islamic terrain, I might be disappointed by all the patriarchy I'd find there. I am so weary of finding it in my own tradition, I wasn't sure I could handle it in another. One way to avoid it, I decided, was to gather the stories of women. (See p. 48.)

2. Throughout the history of the church, its priests, pastors, biblical interpreters, and theologians have been predominantly male. Islam has a similar history. In spite of the predominance of men, is it possible to learn about faith through the eyes of the women in the church? Who have been important female voices in your faith formation? And how have they shaped you?

"Saying Islam meaningfully," writes Shahab Ahmed in his book *What Is Islam?*, "requires making ourselves sensitive to the 'capaciousness, complexity and, often outright contradiction' that inheres within the broadest possible range of practices, beliefs, representational forms, metaphors, and objects associated with Islam." (See p. 50.)

3. Just as Christianity is complex and diverse, full of people who may feel very differently about political, social, and aesthetic issues, so is Islam. Is the diversity, the capaciousness, apparent to people who do not identify with these faiths? How is it represented in popular culture? What happens when something is viewed as monolithic rather than complex?

His youngest wife, Aisha, was "brilliant and feisty," according to Hend. She lived for forty-four years after Muhammad died and was instrumental in collecting the hadith, the sayings or narratives about Muhammad's words and deeds not included in the Qur'an but essential to informing Islamic law. . . . In many respects, Aisha is the most important person in the development of the hadith. A woman. (See pp. 53–54.)

4. Though it's possible that there were women involved in the holy writings of the Jewish and Christian traditions, we don't have any stories to indicate that this might be the case. Does this make the story of Aisha's central role in collecting the hadith seem significant or surprising? How so?

Chapter Five
Full Faith and Effort:
Where I Meet a Feminist Muslim Scholar

In the Qur'an both sexes are created deliberately and independently. There is no mention of Eve being created out of Adam's rib. And Adam is as much the first sinner as Eve. The Qur'an clearly establishes the equality of men and women. Surah 3:195 says, "I shall not lose sight of the labor of any of you who labors in My way, be it man or woman; each of you is equal to the other." (See p. 59.)

1. Many Christians believe in the equality of men and women; nevertheless, Christianity has a history of excluding women from leadership roles on the basis of the story of Adam and Eve (as well as the story of Jesus). If the biblical text were more explicit about the equality of the sexes, how would it make a difference?

In Islamic tradition, Hagar's expulsion from Abraham's household isn't an episode of female oppression; it is a part of God's plan to establish a sanctuary in the desert along with rituals that pilgrims will follow as long as the world endures. (See p. 61.)

2. The Islamic way of reading Hagar's story differs from what we encounter in Judaism or Christianity. It gives Hagar more power—she is not a victim, but a heroine. Can the lens with which we view Hagar shift independently of the tradition to which we adhere? Can the Islamic way of telling the story influence how other traditions read the story? Or is that somehow off-limits? How would it influence your own reading of Hagar?

If you die never having followed in Hagar's footsteps, your kids can do it for you. If you are too poor, someone can make the hajj on your behalf. If you are not at the hajj because you have already gone, you still celebrate what the pilgrims there are doing. So every single year you're talking about Hagar, thinking about what she did. You are remembering her story. (See p. 63.)

3. Anse Tamara Gray (the feminist Muslim scholar) cherishes the fact that all Muslims, regardless of gender, must imitate a woman if they hope to complete the five pillars of Islam. Does this seem significant to you? How might the practice of following in the steps of a woman make a difference in the life of a faith? Are there women from your tradition whom you embrace in this way or whose stories you remember in a certain season?

The text points out that these are all Islamic head coverings. A Nigerian woman wears a colorful kerchief in bold African print tied around her head. It matches her dress. A young girl from Kazakhstan models a very cute hat, like one missionaries brought back to my parents when I was a child. . . . Another image shows a woman from Bulgaria with a scarf tied under her chin—an Eastern European look. Looking at these pictures . . . made me realize how little I know about so many things and how important it is to remember that. (See pp. 66–67.)

4. Whatever tradition we come from, we likely have assumptions about other religious traditions. What are some of your assumptions?

5. Are there things about your religious practice that outsiders might see as oppressive, but that you don't necessarily experience that way? If so, give a few examples.

6. Have you encountered images, or people, or words that have changed your perspective or made you suddenly realize how little you know? What were these encounters like?

Chapter Six
Iftar:
Visiting a Mosque with my Daughter

I know nothing is ever uncomplicated, but focusing on the mother can shift the way we read our sacred stories—make a way when it seems like there is no way. (See p. 73.)

1. What are some of the complications of focusing on the mother?

2. Have you experienced worship outside of your own tradition? What was the experience like for you?

3. Is there sometimes a difference in places where two or more women are gathered versus two or more men? If so, can you describe the difference?

Part Three: Esther

Chapter Seven
The Biblical Story:
The Jewish Heroine Who Reclaims Eros

Characters in the Bible may reveal a truth about the human condition or what it's like to be a human in relationship with God. They are inspirational at times. But as for figures we're meant to emulate? David slept with another man's wife and proceeded to have the man killed. Ezekiel ate a scroll and lay on his left side for 390 days. Hosea named his children "Unloved" and "Not My People." The disciples betrayed Jesus at his most crucial hour. The characters in the Bible are wonderfully and terribly human. (See p. 78.)

1. Do you agree with the author's evaluation of characters in the Bible, or are there some you look to as role models? Which ones?

Maimonides, a medieval Sephardic Jewish philosopher and foremost commentator on the Torah, says that in the age to come, when the light of the Messiah shines unobstructed, when the books of the prophets and the other sacred writings have been suspended—when they cease to be read in public, the scroll of Esther will continue to have vitality. Ancient troubles will be remembered no more, but the days of Purim, the festival of Esther, will be celebrated into infinity. (See p. 80.)

2. After reading chapter 7, why do you think Maimonides argues that Esther will continue to have vitality when other scriptural writing ceases to be relevant?

We need her in our triumvirate—for all the lipstick-loving, high-heel-wearing, anti-sex-shaming, sex-positive advocates—for those seeking relief from patriarchal strictures on women's sexuality—for every woman ever called a slut. It's surprising and refreshing to meet such a woman in the pages of our holy book. (See p. 82.)

3. People are divided on Esther—she is both shunned and embraced. What are your feelings about Esther as a character? She uses her beauty and sexuality to convince the king not to kill her people. How does this strike you?

4. Consider Esther alongside the #MeToo movement. What questions arise? Did Esther have agency? Did she act freely?

After those self-important men comes a book about a woman—who without the help of father or brother or husband—without being pure or holy or virginal, stands in the eye of an ego-driven, farcical, man-made nearly catastrophic storm, and acts to save her people from destruction. (See p. 86.)

5. The men in Esther (from Mordecai to Haman) behave in ways that are both foolish and destructive, and it is a woman who averts disaster—but, of course, women can be ego-driven as well as men. Are there examples from your own life, or popular culture, or current events where you have noticed ego-driven actions leading in destructive directions? How do you think gender plays a role in this, if it does at all?

Rabbi Spilker keeps posing questions and saying, "These are questions. I'm not answering them." (See p. 91.)

6. When reading a text, how does posing questions that you don't have answers to change the way you think?

7. Try reading Genesis chapter 1, or a chapter from one of the Gospels, and ask whatever questions come into your head without looking for an answer, without even assuming there is an answer. Try this with a group. Take fifteen minutes to ask questions—no answers allowed. Does this open up the text in a different way? Or do you find it frustrating?

It may actually be the absence of God that makes Esther a compelling book for our times. No prophet hears God's voice. God has no instructions or directions or appearances. If God is present, God is hidden. The book of Esther takes place after the major events in biblical history. God doesn't show up in a pillar of fire or at the door of Moses's tent. God's not handing people tablets or revealing an obvious path. This sounds familiar. We may say we hear God's voice in Scripture, or our neighbor, or the poor, but that's a little different than a voice from heaven. Faith includes ambiguity and mystery. (See pp. 93–94.)

8. Some people experience more ambiguity than others in their faith lives. Many people talk about feeling divine direction while some never do. What is your experience like?

9. In what ways and circumstances have you experienced God's absence and/or God's presence in your life?

Christians believe in a God who reveals godself, not in the expected way of the gods—all-powerful and mighty, but in a rather unexpected way—a God who empties godself of power for love, a God who gets a body and dies on the cross. In the midrash Esther prays the words of Psalm 22, "My God, my God why hast thou forsaken me?" That was the same prayer Jesus prayed on the cross, according to the Gospels. This is not a warrior-god armed for battle. (See pp. 96–97.)

10. How do you define power? Perhaps Christ doesn't so much give up power as he empties it of what it usually means and fills it with something else. Love is powerful. Grief is powerful. But in very different ways than armies or presidents are powerful. What do you think of power? Is it something we need?

Chapter Eight
Purim:
The Farce Awakens

I tell her I'm a pastor from a Lutheran congregation. She says she doesn't know much about Christianity and asks me what beliefs we share. This question makes me nervous. Do I say, "Well, actually, we got everything from you and tried to make it about us," or do I talk about love, and grace, and justice? Or is she just testing me to see if I can handle it? More than anything, I feel like apologizing—for supersessionism, and Martin Luther, and Paul, and the Inquisition, and the Holocaust. (See p. 105.)

1. The author recognizes how uncomfortable she feels talking about the beliefs Christianity and Judaism share—as if "share" isn't quite the right word for how Christianity relates to Judaism. What do you think?

2. How do you feel when you talk about your faith with people who identify with a different tradition? What do you think makes these conversations difficult, or not, depending on how you feel?

As I was scanning the Internet for Purim celebrations, I saw there was a Twin Cities–wide Purim after-party in 2013 called Cirque Du Purim, which featured fire jugglers, stilt walkers, and DJ Becca Gee "spinning sick beats." This year the same organization is throwing a party, and the invitation says, "Yes, we know it's a weeknight. Yes, we know it's late. But it's Purim, people! This only happens once a year! It's your religious OBLIGATION to party like it's 5776." (See p. 110.)

3. The author's experience of Purim is mostly one of celebration and humor, although some of the humor is pointed, and there's definitely an element of resistance to power. The celebrations aren't focused on the danger or tragedy of genocide. How do comedy and tragedy relate?

4. Perhaps there are times when being an insider or an outsider does determine how you are permitted to relate to something. Often things that are okay to joke about or say inside a family are not okay for nonfamily members to say. Have you experienced this dynamic? In what circumstances?

Amidst farcical, terrible, and unprecedented events, who knows? Maybe you are here at such a time as this for a reason. (See p. 113.)

5. Mordechai doesn't give Esther a directive. Instead, he poses a question: "Who knows?" And yet the question is a powerful one—more pressing, perhaps, than a directive. Do you know for certain why you are here or what you should do? If you don't know for certain, how do you proceed in these circumstances?

Chapter Nine
Shoah:
Scapegoating and Status-Seeking

> The Christian tradition has often been more oriented toward answers. It is not uncommon to hear Christians say, "Jesus is the answer." But like the Jewish rabbis, Jesus asks more questions than he answers. "Who do you say that I am?" "What is it you want?" "Why are you so afraid?" (See p. 115.)

1. Why do you think Jesus asks so many questions? Is it important to you to assert that he is the answer to your questions, or are there other ways you could look at it?

> Though the Christian faith, obviously, came from Judaism and owes its life to it, Christianity has a long and shameful history of anti-Semitism. You can see a growing combativeness toward Jewish people who do not accept Jesus as the Messiah almost right off the bat. If you read the book of Acts as a Christian, it's a story of how the gospel spread. If you read it as a Jewish person, well, by chapter 3, Peter is accusing the men of Israel of murdering the author of life. (See p. 117.)

2. Read Acts 3:11–26. Do you see Peter delineating an "us" and a "them"? Or is he just proclaiming what he believes is the "good news"? How do you see the relationship between Judaism and Christianity?

> It seems like a sort of cheap criticism really—like making fun of people for what they wear. What's wrong with phylac-

teries? You take a little leather box, and you roll up a piece of parchment with words from Scripture written on it: "You shall love the Lord your God with all your heart and all your soul and all your mind," and you put the piece of parchment in the box, and you fasten it on your hand or your head to remind you that these words shall be in your heart—they shall be a frontlet between the eyes and a token on your hand. I mean, yes, it might look a little odd to wear a small box on your forehead or your hand—but what about that instead of smartphones fastened to our hands and heads—to remind us of the forces that guide us? (See p. 121.)

3. Jesus questions some religious traditions. He is attuned to hypocrisy, but does he mean for his followers to abandon meaningful practices? How do you navigate the territory between hypocrisy and meaningful ritual?

4. Perhaps twenty-first-century culture could benefit from a few Sabbath laws to help us pay more attention to stopping, pausing, and ceasing to exert our force on the world. What do you think?

5. Rituals can help us pay attention to what is crucial to life. Rituals can also become burdensome or meaningless. Do you have rituals that give you life? Ones that take life away? What are they?

The midrash is wild and playful—for the rabbis it was a way of "seeking God in their midst," not a way to find some sort of static, rigid, singular answer or formula for living. Questions, for the rabbis, are more important than the answers.

I hope someday to learn to read with the imagination that the spirit of the rabbinic inquiry embodies. (See pp. 122–23.)

6. Does biblical interpretation as a way of seeking God make sense to you? It isn't quite the same as looking for answers in the text. How might the process look different?

7. If we approach a text believing it is possible to find the one correct interpretation, we will approach it differently than if we allow for a multiplicity of readings. What are the advantages and drawbacks of these different approaches?

I'm pretty sure that if there's good news in this text, it is that whoever exalts himself will be humbled and whoever humbles himself will be exalted. Maybe that's a beautiful promise—though it's not exactly cupcakes and ice cream. (See p. 125.)

8. What leads people to exalt themselves at the expense of others? Fear? Arrogance? Are the two things related?

9. What might be beautiful about these sorts of reversals (where the humbled are exalted and the exalted humbled)? What might make them painful? Have you experienced being humbled or exalted in a way that is freeing or difficult?

Part Four: Mary

Chapter Ten
The Biblical Story:
The Subversive Mother of God

> But however much the Baptist church managed to diminish her role, there's no getting around this beautiful and stunning fact: amidst all the pages of patriarchy, the gospel of Jesus Christ begins with the Beloved Mother—a woman who gives birth to God. (See p. 130.)

1. Is the author making too much of Mary's presence in the gospel, or do you see it as significant?

> Mary doesn't immediately agree to this. "He whom the entire universe could not contain" will be contained in her womb (as an ancient hymn puts it). Naturally, she asks, "How can this be?" Certainly Mary couldn't understand how all this worked (who could?) but she agrees to be a part of it. Meek wouldn't be a word I'd choose for her. "Hail Mary, full of grace," the angel says—full of grace, God's most stunning attribute. She's named after Miriam, who coleads the Exodus and whose name means *rebel*.

> A powerless teenage girl overcome unwillingly by the Spirit of God? I wouldn't put it that way. A subversive who somehow makes her way into the Vatican and onto the mantels of fundamentalist households in a Christmas crèche in Texas and Tennessee? Maybe that's more like it. (See p. 133.)

2. Have you experienced Mary as a powerful woman or a powerless girl? How have communities that you are a part of portrayed her?

> God becomes physical, embodied, given flesh in Mary. There's no denying it's an outrageous story, with all its scandalous specificity. God comes into the world, like all mammals, as a cluster of cells attached to the uterine wall nourished by the placenta, and will be fed from the milk of Mary's breasts. It's God mixed up in the molecules of life. Mary has a way of keeping things grounded. (See p. 136.)

3. So far, humans experience life in bodies. Do you think it's possible that human life could exist in some other form? Virtual reality, artificial intelligence, and other technological developments look different from ancient Gnosticism, but is there something that we're grasping after in our technological advancements that is similar?

4. Does the incarnation seem scandalous to you? In what ways? Why might keeping a faith grounded in this belief be important? What are the implications for practice?

> In this first glimpse we have of Jesus's mother in the Gospel of John, the first words she utters are "They have no wine." It's almost like a lament. The only other time we encounter her in this book is at the foot of the cross on which her son dies. It's like she appears at the archetypal moments of human anxiety: death and the moment the wine runs out. (See p. 141.)

5. Luke spends much more time on Mary than the other Gospels do. What might have been at play in the various authors' decisions to downplay or feature her? Do you find Mary's appearances in the Gospel of John to be significant? Why or why not?

> The cross is the story of how Jesus participates in human suffering, and it reveals that God is present in our pain and sorrow, but I'm not sure we're always able to feel how Jesus suffered. Perhaps we can't quite relate to Jesus's suffering because he's God incarnate, he died to save the world, we're told, he's a martyr on a cross—he's not like us. But Mary's suffering is visceral for us. She watches her son die. (See p. 143.)

6. Many Christians across time have looked to Mary and prayed to Mary as one who understands suffering and cares for the least. Have you felt connected to Mary in this way? Why or why not?

7. In his 2018 New Year's address, Pope Francis said that, "Devotion to Mary is not spiritual etiquette; it is a requirement of the Christian life . . . the gift of the Mother . . . is most precious for the church. If our faith is not to be reduced merely to an idea or a doctrine, all of us need a mother's heart, one which knows how to keep the tender love of God and to feel the heartbeat of all around us." What do you think of the pope's statement?

> We need a lot of help here on this broken planet. I believe in the grace of God. But when children die, and teenagers

are shot by police, and the entire Caribbean is ravaged by unprecedented hurricane damage, and the people who always get hit hard are getting hit harder, and a friend loses her twenty-two-year-old son, I don't know how the aggrieved are supposed to muster Hagar's effort. Or Esther's charms. We need their stories to give us hope and strength and ideas for resistance, but at times we are so sad, and sick, and weary that we need to be able to lie down and find rest in the arms of a mother who knows suffering, who is so well acquainted with grief[,] . . . the woman clothed with the sun . . . (See pp. 146–47.)

8. We may long for a god who can keep us from suffering, and yet people still suffer from violence, displacement, hunger, racism, disease, poverty—the list is long. Climate change will result in flooding and natural disasters will disproportionately affect the already impoverished. What does faith mean in these times and situations? Do you believe God is with us? In what way is God with us?

Chapter Eleven
The Shape-Shifting Queen:
Goddesses, Guadalupe, and Grandmas

Lots of stories circulated about Jesus—his birth, and life, and death. And there were many stories about his mother. The stories that the community eventually deemed reliable or important were made canonical. But most of the stories of Mary remain outside the official narratives—pre-canon, post-canon, in apocryphal writing in every century: in Medjugore, Fatima, and Lourdes, in Poland, Rwanda, Egypt, and China. Authorities never successfully regulated her. People have never stopped talking about her, having visions of her, and being healed and comforted by her. (See p. 150.)

1. The shared stories of a canon are important, but this doesn't mean there isn't value to unofficial narratives that move outside established boundaries. What are the merits of the canonical and the noncanonical?

The versions of Mary are vast, and however much the imperial version may have tried to make itself the one true version, it never worked. Mary is Our Lady of Grace, Compassion, Light, Sorrows, Mercy, Guidance, the Daughter of Zion, Seat of Wisdom, Refuge of Sinners, Mirror of Justice, Queen of Peace, Star of the Sea, Mystical Rose. (See p. 157.)

2. Of course, the members of the Trinity are known by many names as well. Why the proliferation of names and images?

In Sicily a statue of Mary is covered in flowers and paraded through the streets. A facing procession carries a statue of Jesus. When they meet they bow three times to each other. In Italy people carry bowls of rosewater, which they sprinkle on themselves, and they throw coins out of windows. In Brazil pageants are held on decorated canoes. There's a blessing of the Alps in Austria.

Mary is a bridge: pre-Christian practice merging with church-sanctioned festivities. Is the church co-opting lo-

cal Indigenous goddesses (Isis, Brigid, Tonantzin, Coatlicue, Diana), or are the goddesses just quietly crossing the
bridge? (See p. 159.)

3. For many Christians throughout history, "goddess" has been
considered a pagan, or dangerous, or silly word. We have seen
throughout this book some reasons why monotheism might
have shunned the goddess. Do you think there is room for her
or a need for her in Abrahamic monotheism? What do you
think about mixing indigenous belief with orthodox belief?

The Zapatistas, the Sandinistas, and the United Farm
Workers emblazoned her image on flags, and standards,
and T-shirts as they carried out their struggles for justice
against oppressive regimes and corporate abuse. In demonstrations against the criminalization of immigrants, the Virgin of Guadalupe can be seen on the banners of protesters.
Her image is also popular with pro-life groups. (See p. 163.)

4. Jesus also stands for the oppressed, but you would probably
not see his image on the banners of protesters resisting corporate power. What makes Guadalupe a symbol of resistance?

Mary may look a little meek and mild and Italian at the
Vatican, that all-male conclave of officials refining doctrine,
but check her out as a Haitian woman smoking a Marlboro.
Or as a muscular Latina in boxing gloves. She's a wealthy
European aristocrat with a long elegant neck, draped in lush
fabrics. She is a stout peasant with a short waist. Maybe it's
because she so emphatically connects the Christian story
with the physical that she is so variously represented in

physical form. At St. Patrick's Guild Church Supply, you will see her in numbing conformity, but Google images of the Black Madonna—something that helped me have hope for the resistance on one of those long, hot days during the summer of 2017 when the white boys were yet again threatening the life of this planet. It's astounding to survey how Mary has appeared over time—all across the world, shape-shifting in ways that bring life, comfort, or revolution. (See pp. 167–68.)

5. Rebekah, the artist in chapter 11, suggests that images of Jesus are not nearly as diverse as are images of Mary. Is this true in your experience? Why might this be? Obviously, we don't know what Jesus looked like, but how would you depict Jesus? Mary?

Mary is black. She is Mexican. Sometimes she is lily white too. She wears the masks of the Zapatistas, and you can find her tame and deferential at the Catholic bookstore—whenever, wherever, and however she is found, though, she is unfailingly true to her song. She comes for the poor. And the sick. And the wounded. For mothers who have lost their children, the tired and the oppressed. (See p. 170.)

6. Perhaps you are healthy and wealthy and your children (if you have them) are fine and happy. Does Mary speak to you, and how?

Though the feminine face of the divine is sometimes hard to find in the Bible, no one ever succeeded in getting rid of it entirely. Maybe because however much some groups would have liked to get rid of the traces that didn't fit their agenda, some powerful forces just couldn't be completely shoved under the rug—or maybe "powerful" forces isn't a good way to put it—maybe "truths so alive with beauty and vulnerability and the complexity of human be-ing with God" that you couldn't snuff them out. (See p. 172.)

7. The author has tried to make a case for the importance of the feminine face of the divine. She has suggested that focusing on the women in Scripture might create a different lens that could change some of our assumptions (maybe even some of our violence) or our faiths. What do you think?